Enjoying Life
on the INDIAN RIVER LAGOON COAST

Tales from **Florida's** *Greatest Lagoon*

Rodney

by RODNEY SMITH

PURE OCEAN PRODUCTIONS
P.O. Box 373257
Satellite Beach, FL 32937-1257
www.pureoceanproductions.com

ISBN-978-0-9771284-3-3

Cover Design BY NATALIE LOPEZ
Cover Photograph © RODNEY SMITH
Text Design BY NATALIE LOPEZ
Edited BY TARA KILLEN
Printed on acid-free paper

stocks and bonds we might hold with a brokerage firm or with our employer in a savings or stock plan, and equity in a business. Because of the potential importance of these assets for retirement purposes, we will call them Pillar 4 assets. Pillar 4 assets far outweigh the sum of all the assets in the traditional three pillars combined.

Purpose of the Pillars

Here's one way of looking at the role of the four pillars:

- **Pillar 1** (OAS and GIS) ensures that even the least well-off Canadians will have enough money to meet the necessities of life, even if they haven't saved at all for retirement.

- **Pillar 2** (C/QPP) when combined with Pillar 1 elevates retired Canadians from subsistence levels, but the two pillars combined are not enough to replace the living standard they had while they were working. The exception is low-income households who can actually have more disposable income in retirement from Pillars 1 and 2 than they had while they were working.

- **Pillar 3** when combined with Pillars 1 and 2 provides middle- to high-income workers a tax-effective way to save so that they can achieve a standard of living in retirement comparable to the standard they enjoyed while working. Some low-income workers also participate in Pillar 3 retirement vehicles, but this may not be wise since it can reduce their Pillar 1 entitlement.

- **Pillar 4** may be the true source of retirement security for many middle- to high-income workers, especially if they have not been saving through Pillar 3 vehicles.

Figure 2.1: Canada's 3-Pillar Retirement System

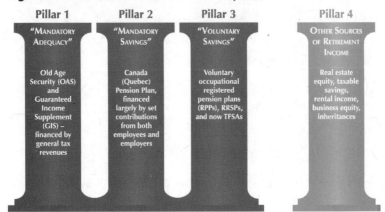

Pillar 1	Pillar 2	Pillar 3	Pillar 4
"MANDATORY ADEQUACY"	"MANDATORY SAVINGS"	"VOLUNTARY SAVINGS"	OTHER SOURCES OF RETIREMENT INCOME
Old Age Security (OAS) and Guaranteed Income Supplement (GIS) – financed by general tax revenues	Canada (Quebec) Pension Plan, financed largely by set contributions from both employees and employers	Voluntary occupational registered pension plans (RPPs), RRSPs, and now TFSAs	Real estate equity, taxable savings, rental income, business equity, inheritances

A Brief History of Retirement Programs in Canada

The pension programs within the three traditional pillars are subject to ongoing adjustments by governments and employers according to the thinking of the day as well as budget constraints and voter pressures. This situation will most certainly continue but the real question is, will future changes within these pillars have a big effect on your retirement planning? Will you need to over-save to prepare for retirement because some programs will be cut back, or can you count on the three pillars to continue more or less in their current form? If we wish to anticipate the future direction of our retirement income system, it helps to review how our current three-pillar system evolved to what it is today.

History of Pillar 1

At the dawn of the twentieth century, Canadians generally had to fend for themselves in retirement. As immigrants and settlers for the most part, they expected and received little in the way of social welfare from government sources or employers. Elderly Canadians who were no longer able to earn their own income had to rely on family members for support and failing that, they had to resort to the poorhouse (a publicly maintained institution).

It wasn't until 1927 that the federal government introduced the Old Age Pensions Act, the first formal program to support the elderly. This act provided a benefit of $20 each month to British subjects who were 70 years of age or older and who had been residents of Canada for at least 20 years. In addition, their annual income had to be less than $365, and they needed to demonstrate they had no children capable of supporting them.

This program was better than nothing but it received its share of criticism during its relatively short life. The means test, in particular, was a bone of contention because it attached a stigma to receiving payments under the act. As a result, the program was replaced by the Old Age Security (OAS) Act in 1952. Besides increasing payments to $40 monthly, the OAS eliminated the means test for eligibility. At this stage, OAS payments still commenced at age 70.

The Guaranteed Income Supplement (GIS) was introduced in 1966, at about the same time as the Canada Pension Plan. It was initially expected to be a temporary supplement to alleviate widespread poverty among seniors and was not expected to survive once the CPP was fully phased in, which would occur in 1976. Eventually, however, the GIS became a permanent program. Also in 1966, the starting age for OAS was reduced in stages from 70 to 65, to match the starting age for the CPP. The final big change that led to the OAS and CPP resembling the modern-day programs occurred in 1972 with the automatic indexing of benefits to changes in the Consumer Price Index (CPI). The indexation of OAS was changed in 1973 so that benefits payable were adjusted quarterly to changes in the cost of living as measured by the CPI. One last significant change to Pillar 1 was the introduction of a Spouse's Allowance which provided benefits for the spouses of individuals who were receiving GIS.

From 1927 until 1989, Pillar 1 saw only continual improvements. This started to change in 1989 when the much-detested clawback of OAS was introduced. The clawback reduced the OAS pension by 15 per cent of the amount by which a pensioner's net income exceeded a given threshold. This was the government's attempt to control the cost of the OAS program by clawing back a portion of the payments received by higher-income retirees. The other major take-away, which was introduced in the 2012 federal budget, will move the starting age for OAS pension from 65 to 67. This will be phased in gradually between 2023 and 2029. The cost of OAS currently represents about 2.3 per cent of GDP but the chief actuary for the Canada Pension Plan forecasts it would have risen to about 3.1 per cent by 2030 had the retirement age not been increased.

As of June 2012, the maximum OAS pension is $6,481 a year. Retirees with sufficiently high income will have their OAS payments clawed back to the extent their net income exceeds $69,562. That means that one's OAS benefits shrink incrementally until net income reaches $112,772, at which point the OAS benefits vanish entirely. The income thresholds for the clawback change annually with inflation.

The maximum GIS payment is $8,788 a year for a single pensioner and $11,654 a year in the case of a couple that both receive OAS. When combined with OAS, a retired couple can receive $24,616 in annual pension before considering any additional pension they might get from the other pillars. For the lowest 20 per cent of income-earners, this is more than couples were earning in employment income before they retired.

It is important to note that Pillar 1 is fundamentally different from Pillars 2 and 3 in that it is the only pillar where the cost is paid by the government. Pillars 2 and 3 are funded solely by employee and employer contributions. For this reason, the government is more likely to cut back on Pillar 1 benefits if and when it faces a financial crunch rather than on Pillars 2 or 3.

History of Pillar 2

The Canada Pension Plan (CPP), which is an earnings-related universal program funded by employers and employees, was a long time in coming. Germany has had a social security program funded by employers and employees since 1889 and even the U.S., which is usually regarded as a more laissez-faire nation, had established a social security system in 1935. The Canadian Labour Congress had been calling for a universal and publicly administered earnings-related system for Canada since 1953. One of the hurdles to overcome was the challenge of getting all the provinces onside. An incentive to gain the consent of the provinces was that the contributions into the CPP would be loaned back to the provinces at a favourable rate of interest and would not have to be repaid for decades, if ever, as long as the monies going into the CPP exceeded the benefits being paid out.

The CPP finally came into being in 1966 and covered essentially all workers between the ages of 18 and 70. Quebec insisted on having its own program, the Quebec Pension Plan (QPP), as a means of allowing the Quebec government to control pension fund reserves for investment in provincial development. (Other provinces also had the option of establishing their own parallel plans, but chose not to do so.)

The C/QPP started as a pay-as-you-go plan with the very low contribution rate by both employees and employers of just 1.9 per cent of earnings up to a modest ceiling. The trouble with pay-as-you-go plans is that the contribution rate keeps on climbing as the plan matures and can eventually reach intolerably high levels. This could be avoided by funding the benefits in advance but this raises new problems such as finding enough investments generating good returns with such an enormous sum. The compromise that was reached was to partly fund the C/QPP. Starting in 1995, the contribution rate was ramped up in stages to 4.95 per cent of pensionable earnings on the part of both employees and employers, which means the combined contribution rate is 9.9 per cent. This was deemed to be enough to keep the C/QPP 20 per cent funded over the long term. The fact that the C/QPP will remain 80 per cent unfunded sounds rather alarming but it shouldn't be. The 20 per cent funded level is enough to avoid any future escalation of the contribution rate, assuming the capital markets and demographics co-operate.

Things have worked out well for the CPP since this funding solution was implemented. The 9.9 per cent contribution rate is considered to be sustainable for at least the next 75 years. It has worked out less well in Quebec because factors such as plummeting fertility rates, high unemployment rates, and sub-optimal immigration rates have caused the long-term cost to rise to about 11.2 per cent of pay.

The basic pension formula under the C/QPP is a target pension of 25 per cent of employment earnings up to a ceiling. The earnings ceiling was very low in the early years of the program, but is now equal to the average national wage. Someone who earns the average national wage, which is currently at about $50,000, can expect an annual pension of just under $12,000. It is not quite 25 per cent of the earnings ceiling because it is averaged over the final three years. The pension can be less if one had a significant number of years with no earnings or low earnings between age 18 and retirement.

Unlike the OAS and GIS programs, which saw a series of improvements in the early years, the C/QPP has not undergone any significant improvement apart from the addition of some flexibility to the pension commencement age. Since 1987, new retirees under the C/QPP could start their pension as early as 60, subject to a penalty, and as late as 70, in which case the pension payable would be increased.

There have been some minor take-aways under the C/QPP over the years, such as changing the earnings base for pension calculation purposes from an average of the final three years' earnings ceiling to an average of five years. This was necessary to keep the cost under the 9.9 per cent ceiling. Another take-away, which is being phased in between 2012 and 2016, will result in smaller pensions before age 65 but this is balanced by larger pensions when the starting age is between ages 65 and 70. Like OAS and GIS, both the CPP and QPP are indexed to provide protection against inflation. The difference is that the indexation under the C/QPP occurs annually rather than quarterly.

Figure 2.2 summarizes the evolution of pension benefits payable monthly under Pillars 1 and 2 with the amounts converted into constant 2011 dollars. The amount of pension payable under Pillars 1 and 2 has more than doubled in real terms since 1970. The small dip from 1995 to 2005 is due to the OAS clawback, which was not reflected in OAS pensions payable before 2002. Note the average amount of C/QPP pension paid also dipped in 2000 and 2005. This is because of the increasing number of Canadians who took their C/QPP pensions early and thus received smaller pensions.

Figure 2.2: Historical Pillar 1 and Pillar 2 Benefits (Monthly)

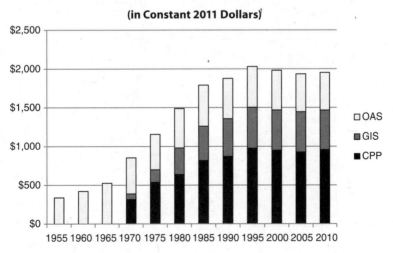

(in Constant 2011 Dollars)

History of Pillar 3

Pillar 3 barely existed half a century ago. Retirement preparation, if any, was expected to occur outside of any tax-assisted retirement vehicles, which might help to explain why the assets in the unofficial fourth pillar are still so important to so many Canadians in helping them supplement their retirement incomes.

The first workplace pension plans in Canada were established in the early twentieth century by railroads and banks, but only a tiny fraction of Canadians were covered. Changing employers prior to retirement age usually meant losing all the pension benefits that one had built up. This draconian rule reflected the consensus at the time that pensions were a reward for long service rather than a form of deferred compensation. These early programs were introduced by employers to manage their workforce. Companies didn't want their retirees coming back to them after they had retired with pleas for financial assistance.

Workplace defined benefit pension plans grew rapidly in the 1960s and 1970s, but by the 1980s employers started having second thoughts about them. A round of pension reform in the late 1980s made these plans much more onerous to manage and employers were disenchanted that they couldn't freely access the surplus that was emerging in these plans as a result of better-than-expected investment returns. By the early 1990s, workplace defined benefit pension plans within the private sector started a long, slow decline into oblivion. Lower interest rates made these plans more expensive than they used to be, and evolving accounting rules made the pension cost much more volatile. The low-interest-rate environment might eventually go away but the accounting problem probably will remain.

Based on the most recent statistics, just 22 per cent of workers in the private sector are covered by workplace pension plans.

Only 16 per cent are covered by defined benefit pension plans, which are the type of plan that protect employees from investment and longevity risk. That is the lowest coverage rate in half a century. The future of employer-sponsored pension plans within Pillar 3 is in some doubt.

Registered Retirement Savings Plans (RRSPs), which enabled individuals to save and manage assets for their retirement years on a tax-assisted basis, were introduced in 1957. Not only are RRSP contributions deductible from earned income for income tax purposes, the investment income that accumulates over time is not subject to income tax until withdrawn. RRSPs were not especially popular when they were first introduced. Even by 1968, the first year data was available on the number of contributors, only 2 per cent of all tax-filers were contributing. That number gradually rose and peaked at 30 per cent by 1997. This might not sound high, but given that (a) tax-filers include retirees, (b) low-income workers are better off not contributing to RRSPs, and (c) many other people participate in workplace pension plans, a 30 per cent coverage rate is fairly high. The participation rate has declined a little since 1997 as the proportion of retirees in the population has increased. The current high cost of home ownership may also be a factor.

Other vehicles within the Pillar 3 designation include Deferred Profit Sharing Plans (DPSPs) and Tax-Free Savings Accounts (TFSAs). DPSPs must be sponsored by an employer, and distributions are made to participating employees out of profits. These plans are relatively rare; only a very small fraction of Canadians are covered by DPSPs. TFSAs represent voluntary arrangements for individuals and in some cases serve as a viable alternative to RRSPs. In some ways, RRSPs and TFSAs are diametrically opposed: with RRSPs, money is not taxed going in, but is taxed when withdrawn; with TFSAs, the reverse is true. TFSAs, introduced in January 2009, are too new and the contribution limits too low (currently $5,000 annually) to have had much impact yet on retirement savings. Most likely, they will grow in popularity as appreciation for their specific advantages grows, much like what happened with RRSPs in the 1960s and 1970s.

The Apparent Problem of Low Coverage

In any given year, only 50 per cent of tax-filers contribute to an RRSP or participate in a pension plan. Since RRSPs and pension plans make up the lion's share of Pillar 3, this low participation rate suggests that Pillar 3 rests on shaky ground. To the extent Canadians agree we have a pension crisis, this is the crux of it; this explains why pension experts keep warning us that Canadians are not saving enough for retirement.

Is the problem as serious as they say? So far, the answer appears to be no. Lower-income Canadians have been able to retire and maintain their living standard with the combination of OAS, GIS, and some C/QPP pension. Most middle- and upper-income Canadians have also retired fairly comfortably, either because they were part of the lucky minority that had substantial Pillar 3 retirement income, or because they sidestepped Pillar 3 and built up their Pillar 4 assets, from which they are now drawing income. While some people are falling through the cracks—primarily single, middle-income people with no Pillar 3 or Pillar 4 assets—they represent a small fraction of all retirees to date. Whatever steps are taken to improve their situation, we need to be careful not to end up forcing others to over-save.

The Long Goodbye to Defined Benefit Pensions

Workplace defined benefit (DB) pension plans hold a special place within Pillar 3. Once the backbone of Pillar 3, these are plans in which the pension benefit is defined by a formula that usually relates to service and possibly earnings. Because the benefit is fixed (i.e., the amount of the pension received by the retiree in these plans does not change based on changes in investment returns), the cost to fund the plan will vary for a number of reasons, but especially because the discount rates used to determine the liabilities will change and the investment returns on the pension fund assets will generate both gains and losses over time. It is the losses that present the problem. Wild swings in DB plan funding costs have presented a major challenge for private sector companies.

Through the 1970s and 1980s, DB plans represented the standard for employee retirement programs. Regardless of the actual returns on their investment, employers guaranteed a benefit, usually for life, so in addition to the risk that the fund's investments might perform below expectations, employers bore all of the longevity risk for their employees (i.e., if retirees live longer than expected, the benefit still continues).

Companies hate financial surprises because of the flak they end up receiving from investors, and the investment and longevity risks have generated their share of nasty surprises over the years. The solution was for employers to abandon DB plans in favour of defined contribution (DC) pension plans in which the employer contribution is fixed at a given percentage of pay. There are no surprises for the company or its shareholders, but that is because all of the risk is shifted to employees whose pensions are no longer fixed. Rather, the pension is whatever income can be generated from the member's account balance at retirement, which is another way of saying that employees assume both the investment risk and the longevity risk.

Other countries, led by the United States and United Kingdom, have seen similar shifts from DB to DC plans. The migration to DC started in the U.S. in the mid-1980s. In 1985, DB plans represented 65 per cent of all plans, but that share dropped to 40 per cent by 2005. The real shift is even more pronounced because about half of the DB plans in the U.S. are closed to new members. In the U.K., the majority of the shifts have occurred since 2000. The U.K.'s Government Actuary's Department reported that DB plan membership declined from 5.16 million to 3.66 million between 1995 and 2005. In Canada, the shift from DB to DC plans is less pronounced, because the public sector staunchly remains DB and accounts for over half of all the active members in pension plans. Still, the drop in the private sector coverage from 26 per cent in 1991 to 16 per cent in 2011 is very significant. Details are given in Table 2.1, which is derived from a Statistics Canada report.

Table 2.1: Change in Pension Coverage for Canadian Employees, 1991 and 2006[1]

(All Figures in 1,000s)	1991	2006
All Sectors		
Employees	11,672	15,043
DB plan members	4,773 (41%)	4,581 (36%)
DC plan members	466 (4%)	899 (6%)
Public Sector		
Employees	2,855	3,262
DB plan members	2,464 (86%)	2,551 (78%)
DC plan members	81 (3%)	132 (4%)
Private Sector		
Employees	8,815	11,781
DB plan members	2,310 (26%)	2,031 (17%)
DC plan members	385 (4%)	767 (7%)

Note that almost four out of five members in the public sector are enrolled in DB plans, compared to just one out of six employees in the private sector.

Many observers believe the shift to DC plans is short-sighted—that we will face enormous social problems as people retire with inadequate savings because of their low savings rate, poor investment choices, and higher management costs within DC arrangements. Given other findings within this book, this view seems unduly alarmist and in any event, at least one outcome is not in dispute: Canadians will have to take greater responsibility for their own retirement.

Where the Retirement System is Trending

Having set in motion an unpopular take-away by moving the retirement age for OAS and GIS benefits to 67, the government is unlikely to impose any more negative changes to these programs in the foreseeable future. The income threshold for the OAS clawback could have been lowered perhaps, but the fact it didn't happen at the same time means it is not likely. This isn't to say that the retirement age for OAS and GIS won't eventually become 69, or that the clawback threshold won't be lowered; it just won't happen for quite some time.

Within Pillar 3, Pooled Registered Pension Plans (PRPPs) could overtake employer-sponsored plans as the primary retirement vehicle in the workplace. Essentially, PRPPs are like RRSPs, except that employees are automatically enrolled and need to take action to opt out. PRPPs are government-sponsored plans, although not government-run, and employers are only involved to the extent they select the PRPP provider and make the necessary payroll deductions. Their attraction for employers is that the employer has no legal liability and is almost totally off the hook in terms of managing the plans. PRPPs are expected to become available in 2013. If they prove to be popular, the twentieth-century experiment with employer-sponsored plans as the keystone of Pillar 3 may come to an end.

While further changes to Pillar 1 (OAS and GIS) are not in the offing, spending on Pillar 1 pensions will decline for another reason. By promoting PRPPs, the government will be helping low-income Canadians build up their retirement savings. This sounds like a good thing, but it comes at a high price for some. If PRPPs are successful in signing up low-income Canadians, the higher retirement income they get will be partly offset by a smaller GIS benefit. Without knowing it, low-income Canadians will be hurting themselves by participating in PRPPs.

The government will have less incentive to reduce benefits under the C/QPP as long as the current funding rate is sustainable. We are assured that the 9.9 per cent funding rate for the CPP is indeed sustainable over the next 75 years. That means that the normal retirement age may remain 65, even though it is scheduled to increase to 67 for OAS purposes. The range of allowable retirement ages might change, though. If we do end up having a major labour shortage as the baby boomers start to retire in large numbers, the government could conceivably change the earliest age for pension commencement under the C/QPP from 60 to 62, for example. It seems hugely inconsistent that the government would raise the C/QPP early retirement age at the same time that they continue to incur enormous costs to provide unreduced early retirement benefits to civil servants, but that is certainly a possibility.

One potential change that has been constantly in the news in recent years is the possible expansion of the C/QPP. This is regularly promoted by labour, the NDP, and the Ontario Liberal government as the most effective solution to the pension coverage problem. An expansion could take a couple of different forms. One is a raising of the earnings ceiling for the plan, which is currently $50,100, to $75,000, or even higher, with the pension benefit remaining at 25 per cent. The other type of expansion is to leave the ceiling the same but to increase the benefit from 25 per cent of earnings to 40 or even

50 per cent. The immediate problem with either form of expansion is that Alberta and Quebec are both opposed to the idea and are big enough to block it. Even if Alberta and Quebec were onside, the other concern with an expansion is that we would be putting too many eggs in one basket. As we have seen, Canada has a three-pillar system, but a major expansion of Pillar 2 will almost certainly result in a shrivelling up of Pillar 3, which practically takes the private sector out of the pension business.

We are confident that a three-pillar system of some sort will remain intact, if only because it has already withstood the test of time. Core benefits from Pillar 1 will remain secure for those with limited means, although payment of pensions will start later. The retirement system may expect those with high income to take on even more individual responsibility for their own welfare. The system will also expect low-income Canadians to do more, given the increase in the OAS retirement age and the fact that PRPPs will surreptitiously cut into GIS benefits.

In summary, the foundation of our retirement system remains strong. There are cracks, but they appear to be manageable. Your retirement security is not likely to be jeopardized in any major way by government actions, but you need to be prepared to cope with a series of relatively minor changes.

3

Understanding the Foundation—Health Care

One might well ask why a book on retirement also looks at Canada's healthcare system. The answer is that health care is such a big-ticket item that expected increases in the cost of health care may very well crowd out spending by governments and employers on pensions. This was one of the reasons given by the government in its 2012 federal budget for upping the retirement age for OAS and GIS benefits to 67.

Canada pays much more for health care than it does for pensions. Even if the OAS program was totally eliminated, and it won't be, the government would still have to make extensive cuts in other program spending or impose a series of punishing tax increases to fund the healthcare system in the future if it remains in its current form. We need to understand better what is happening to the healthcare system before we return to retirement issues.

Early Days of Health Care

Whatever we do, we know we are not going to turn back the clock on the notion of a universally accessible and virtually comprehensive system of health care. Just as Canadians were expected to be self-sufficient in securing their retirement needs a century ago, they also had to pay for whatever minimal health care they received. Services provided by local physicians were often paid for with chickens, apples, or whatever other produce the patient could furnish. Most hospitals were charitable institutions, operating to the extent that contributions permitted.

Stories from the past horrify us:

> *Stories abound in this province of manual labourers forced to cope all their working lives with deteriorated joints or debilitating hernias, and farmers who lived for years with unmedicated asthma or unsightly goiters, and pensioners with untreated cataracts or crippling arthritis . . . because pricey surgical procedures or long-term professional care was simply not a viable option for low-income people.*
>
> —Testimony to the 2002 Commission of the
> Future of Health Care in Canada
> (Romanow Commission)

> *Seniors remember what it was like before Medicare, when we put off seeing the doctor as long as possible because our families could not afford to pay. Many of us bear scars from those days when we did not get appropriate and timely care. Families often experienced heavy debts from the costs of hospitalization for serious illnesses or accidents. In many cases, they were forced to sell their homes. Young people put off their extended education (sometimes indefinitely) to go to work to pay off family debts for health care.*
>
> —Testimony to the 2002
> Romanow Commission

One remembers a young mother dying on the steps of a hospital on Grande Prairie while her husband was inside, begging them to admit her. Another young mother had to sell her two cows to pay the hospital bill for her dead baby before the hospital authorities would release the child's body. A Manitoba senior recalls a neighbouring farm woman who was diagnosed with cancer. She knew that in order to get treatment in a hospital her family would have to sell the farm, so she decided to die at home . . . Her suffering lasted for two months, but she saved the family farm.

—Helen Heeney (ed.),
Life Before Medicare: Canadian Experiences
(Toronto: Ontario Coalition of
Senior Citizens' Organizations, 1995)

Before World War II, health care was privately funded and privately delivered. In 1947, the Saskatchewan government introduced a hospital care plan, and by 1961, all provinces and territories agreed to provide publicly funded hospital services. The key initiative that helped shape the level of coverage currently enjoyed by Canadians was the Saskatchewan Medical Care Insurance Act of 1962, which made it the first province to extend public health insurance to cover both physician and hospital services. A consensus began to emerge that this program should be national. The federal Medical Care Act (MCA), passed in 1966, mandated that public hospital insurance extend coverage to all physician services. By 1972, every province and territory had put together a public health insurance program eligible for federal funding under the MCA. In 1984, the Canada Health Act was introduced, mandating the universal, comprehensive Canadian healthcare system.

THE FIVE PRINCIPLES ENSHRINED IN THE CANADA HEALTH ACT

1. **Public Administration.** All administration of provincial health insurance must be done by a public authority on a non-profit basis. All records and accounts must be available to be audited by the public.

2. **Comprehensiveness.** All medically necessary services (primarily physician and healthcare) must be provided.

3. **Universality.** All insured residents must get equal care.

4. **Portability.** Coverage must be transferred anywhere in the country within reasonable waiting periods and extend to living abroad.

5. **Accessibility.** All insured persons must have reasonable access to healthcare facilities; physicians, hospitals, etc. must be provided with reasonable compensation for their services.

Canadians believe that a strong safety net—comprising health care and pensions—is the foundation of a modern society. Yet there is only so much we can afford. The questions then are what combination of spending cuts and tax increases are we prepared to tolerate as program costs continue to rise, and what are the implications for your retirement planning?

While Canada does not have the same problem in the funding of social programs as Greece, Ireland, Spain, and other European states, there is still some cause for concern. Current government expenditures remain manageable, but increases in healthcare spending in the medium term appear unsustainable, and this could affect the funding of public pensions.

In typical Canadian fashion, the country has taken a middle-of-the-road approach to its health and retirement programs: more prudent in the level of benefits than many European countries but more generous than the U.S. Assuming Canadians wish to continue to maintain this balance, how likely are we to do so, given the prospective changes in future demographics?

Let's begin by looking at the evolution of healthcare expenditures from the mid-1970s to 2010. Figure 3.1 shows the change in per capita cost in constant dollars (thereby removing the effects of inflation).

Figure 3.1: Rising Canadian Healthcare Costs

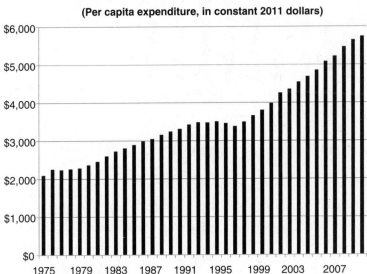

(Per capita expenditure, in constant 2011 dollars)

From a total healthcare expenditure of about $12.2 billion in 1975, representing $527 per capita, Canada spent $192 billion in 2010 for a per capita cost of $5,614, an increase by a factor of more than ten. Had costs simply tracked inflation, the per capita cost in 2010 would have been just $2,050.

Figure 3.2 gives an idea of how the spending by source has changed since 1975. Note that the proportion spent on hospitals has dropped significantly while spending on drugs and capital costs (which include administration costs) has increased.

Figure 3.2: Healthcare Costs by Source, 1975–2010[1]

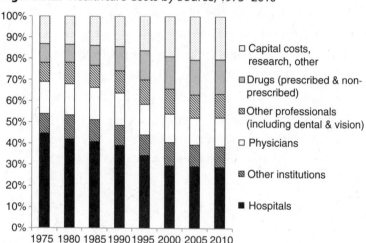

Growing Older and Staying Healthy Is Expensive

What drove the explosion in healthcare costs over this period? Ultimately, it may simply be near-unlimited demand combined with a lack of price resistance, but let's start with a more numerical answer. A recent Canadian Institute for Health Information report broke down the sources of increases from 2000 to 2010 when total health-care spending grew by about 7.4 per cent annually. Price inflation accounted for 1.9 per cent of the annual rise and population growth for another 1 per cent. The aging of the population, which brings higher costs with it, accounted for a surprisingly small 0.8 per cent of the rise. Add up these pieces and we get just 3.7 per cent. The other 3.7 per cent annual increase is attributable to higher utilization, more expensive procedures and drugs, and wage inflation. The last factor is significant. During the period from 2001 to 2009, wages in

Canada as a whole rose by 29 per cent while wages in the healthcare sector rose by 43 per cent. Costs in the health sector cannot outstrip general inflation forever.

Focusing on healthcare costs for seniors, we find they are much more expensive on a per capita basis than the general population, as shown in Figure 3.3.

Figure 3.3: Governmental Healthcare Expenditure (2009)[2]

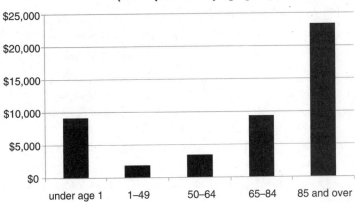

For those unfamiliar with how healthcare costs depend so heavily on age, Figure 3.3 will come as a shock. The per capita cost for those aged 85 and over is more than 12 times as much as for people between ages one and 49.

Canada directs most of its healthcare resources to acute care rather than prevention, which partly explains the extraordinary amounts spent on the elderly. The increasing cost of treating the elderly does not appear to have been a conscious decision by the government or the medical community at large. It simply seems to have evolved on its own because technological progress made it possible. The sidebar, One Physician's Perspective, gives some insight into how it happened.

ONE PHYSICIAN'S PERSPECTIVE

From my experience, 25 years ago the standard tray in an operating room for just about any specialty consisted of a bunch of re-sterilizable stainless steel instruments. Patients stayed in hospital for days or even longer. We eventually got better at treating people as outpatients and saved money on inpatient stays. All those savings have long been factored in and are now overtaken by new costs. New devices, prostheses, and so on are very expensive. Also, the confidence of physicians in doing these procedures on the very old increased. When I was an intern at cardiovascular rounds, we looked at angiograms to decide whether a patient could have a bypass. We never looked at anyone over 70. Now people in their eighties routinely have bypass surgery, angiography, stents, and so on.

An aortic or femoral graft makes repairing aortic aneurysms faster, which results in shorter hospital stays. The graft costs around $20,000 though. The equipment to perform new procedures is far more expensive. In the 1980s I never saw a senior on dialysis but now patients of any age will be dialyzed. A new knee was rare for a senior then; not so, now.

Treating a common condition such as [high] blood pressure is also more expensive because the new drugs cost more. Some studies have suggested that the difference [in result] may not be that great but who's going to deny their patient the best possible care? New drugs for rheumatoid arthritis cost $20,000 a year. Twenty-five years ago patients took a bucket of aspirin.

No one is saying things were better in the old days. On the other hand, it would appear that the cost of new drugs and interventions might be rising more quickly than the incremental improvement in health or life expectancy would justify. It is understandably difficult to apply a hard-nosed cost/benefit analysis in deciding on the type of intervention appropriate in a particular situation. Yet, by avoiding conscious decisions on allocation of resources, we are unconsciously making decisions that will lead to inadequate or delayed care for many.

No Room for More Taxation

As shown in Figure 3.4, Canada's expenditures on health care rose from 7 per cent to almost 12 per cent over the 35 years from 1975 to 2010. That places us near the top of OECD countries in per capita costs, with only the U.S. being appreciably higher. Canada is among the most highly taxed countries in the world, which leaves little room for increased taxation to cover future increases in healthcare costs. Looking at the situation in Canada and other countries (using data provided by the Heritage Foundation in its 2012 Index of Economic Freedom), Canada collects roughly 32.2 per cent of GDP in taxes while the U.S. collects 26.9 per cent, Japan collects 28.3 per cent, and Australia collects 30.8 per cent. European countries collect more, but it's clear that the European model is not working.

Figure 3.4: Health Spending as a Percentage of GDP, 1975–2010

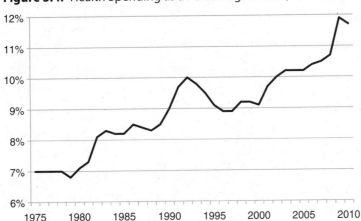

Canada's current fiscal situation is reasonably good, but future increases in government spending cannot do more than track GDP growth if the country is to remain economically and fiscally sound. Instead of expansions of the social safety net, there must be moderate cutbacks in social spending phased in over time—or at least growth that is not in excess of the growth in GDP. Phasing in the eligibility age for OAS and GIS from 65 to 67 is a step in that direction. Introducing pooled registered pension plans (starting in 2013) that will reduce GIS payments to lower-income Canadians is another step. These are still baby steps compared with the type of cuts in spending we need to find within the healthcare sector.

We can expect that government will force Canadians to assume more responsibility for certain healthcare costs. If governments have failed to contain the growth in healthcare expenditures, the obvious solution will be to increase the share of healthcare expenditures borne by individuals. Those likely to be squeezed—or to be provided the option of paying more—are the affluent who, like all Canadians, are currently paying minimal amounts for health care. This will include the better-off retirees.

Some peripheral areas of health care likely to be targeted for more cost shifting are provincial prescription drug plans, living assistance care, nursing home care, and other elderly-specific services. This will have a minimal effect on low-income Canadians as the cost shifting will likely come through means testing or some alternative delivery system. Those with the means to pay can expect to pay more, especially for services not traditionally covered by the public healthcare system. Although coverage of peripheral services is not elderly-specific, the users of these peripheral services are concentrated among the elderly.

Many provinces may institute wider rationing of some preventative diagnostic services such as cancer screening or bone-density tests. Several supportive and rehabilitation services, such as podiatry services, chiropractic services, physiotherapy, acupuncture, psycho-analysis, naturopathy, osteopathy, and prosthetics have limited or no coverage under most provincial health plans, and we should expect any existing coverage to shrink, not widen. Dental, vision, and hearing care, already provided by only a few provinces on a severely limited basis, are likely to become even less available without user fees or some similar charge. Fees are already charged for ambulatory and transportation services in many provinces, and may become more widespread. (It should be noted that these peripheral services are generally provided free of charge to citizens on social assistance.)

Prescription drug costs represent a major healthcare expense. Virtually all provinces have special prescription drug plans for the elderly, and a few have drug plans for all residents. Each province has a list of approved drugs and medical products covered under their respective drug plan, and most plans involve a co-payment charged per prescription along with an annual deductible payment.

No significant changes to provincial drug plans have surfaced in the past few years with the exception of Ontario, which proposed in 2012 to increase charges under its prescription drug plan for high-income seniors. The province's Ontario Drug Benefit (ODB) covers approved drugs for seniors 65 and over, as well as individuals on social assistance and in long-term care facilities, or who are enrolled in home care. A special offshoot of the ODB, called the Trillium Drug Program, covers residents whose drug costs are high relative to their income.

There are many signs, then, that suggest means testing or income testing will be a tool that governments will use more frequently to shift costs toward individuals. While this will not be especially popular with the more affluent, who will be the hardest hit, at least everyone will retain access to services and benefits. This would seem to be the most likely method of achieving social equality and fairness while reducing government costs. It will not be an easy transition, however. Means testing did not go over well early in the twentieth century because it stigmatized the less well off. It led to broad-based support for programs that provided universal, consistent access to comprehensive care, the very programs we can no longer afford.

We'll Need to Start Taking Charge of Our Own Needs

The core of the Canadian healthcare system will remain intact because it is such a high priority for most Canadians. But if governments are unable to contain increases in healthcare costs over the longer term, their only recourse will be to pass along more of those costs to those who can afford to pay, including the more affluent retirees. Middle- and higher-income Canadians cannot count on the status quo. They can expect to be taxed more heavily to fund rising healthcare benefits. They will also be expected to pay more for the same healthcare benefits. As a result, they may need more retirement income than they thought.

4

Our Best Days Are Behind Us

Have you ever had a picture taken of yourself that you thought was unflattering? Then 10 years later you come across that same picture by accident and your first thought is you wished you looked that good now! The Canadian retirement scene is somewhat similar. As we found in Chapter 1, things are better than most of us realize. Despite low levels of participation in pension plans and RRSPs, poverty rates among seniors are much lower than for working-age Canadians. One way or another, most Canadians have found ways to retire with at least adequate retirement income and most recent retirees actually will be able to continue spending as much as they did while working.

But nothing lasts forever, including the happy combination of economic factors that created such a rosy picture for retirees. In fact, some of the factors that created the current positive situation are about to turn against retirees in Canada. The trends have already begun.

The Housing Market's Best Days Are Behind Us

The past 30 years have been a good time to own a home in Canada. In some communities it has been more than good—it has been a bonanza.

Homeowners in the Greater Toronto Area, for example, saw the value of their houses skyrocket about 500 per cent between 1980 and 2010, an astounding development considering that the Consumer Price Index (CPI) rose a modest 154 per cent over the same period. Other markets, most notably Vancouver, saw even bigger percentage increases. Putting it into actual dollars and cents, the value of the equity (i.e., after deducting the mortgage obligation) in privately held residential real estate in this country exceeds all the assets held in the Canada and Quebec Pension Plans, RRSPs, RRIFs, and registered pension plans combined. In other words, the years since 1980 have generated more than an across-the-board improvement in privately held equity; they have created a substantial cushion for retirees.

We are almost certain to witness a much slower increase in real estate values over the next decade or more. The warning signs of this slow-down have already revealed themselves. They include:

- Price increases in the years since 1980 outpaced income growth by a wide margin. In Canada's four largest cities, average incomes rose between 23 per cent and 32 per cent in the fifteen-year period from 1996 to 2009, yet home prices rose between 100 and 200 per cent in the same period—clearly an unsustainable situation.[1]

- The incidence of home ownership among Canadians increased from 64 per cent in 2000 to 70 per cent in 2012, a level that is higher than in the United States when the housing bubble burst in that country in 2006. This is remarkable given that mortgage interest is tax-deductible in the United States but not in Canada. If you isolate the top 50 per cent of income-earners in Canada, more than 90 per cent own their home. The high ownership level means fewer buyers are available to continue pushing prices higher.

- Rents have been rising at a much slower rate than house prices. According to OECD figures from 2008, Canada's house price-to-rent ratio reached an all-time high in that year, placing the country second highest among OECD members. A high house price-to-rent ratio is considered important predictors of future price movements in the housing market.[2] The ratio eventually realigns with historical norms via downward adjustments to house prices rather than an upward movement in rents. This observation was made in a rather prescient commentary[3] on the U.S. housing market in 2004, two years before prices there began their downward slide.

A major impetus for the growth in housing values, especially over the past two decades, has been falling mortgage rates. From a shockingly high 18 per cent[4] in 1982, they dropped steadily to an annual rate of 2.99 per cent for a five-year fixed mortgage in 2012. Mortgage rates affect house prices the same way interest rates affect bonds: when rates fall, prices rise. The monthly payments for a $100,000, 25-year mortgage have fallen from almost $1,500 to under $500. Now that mortgage rates have effectively hit bottom, that particular stimulus to rising home prices is no longer effective.

Low mortgage rates kept the lid on the cost of home ownership even as house prices kept rising to record levels, but that affordability is growing precarious. In spite of those low rates, the average cost of owning a bungalow in Canada in the fourth quarter of 2011 represented 42.2 per cent of pre-tax household income,[5] which equates to 60 per cent or more of after-tax income. The cost for a two-storey home would have been even higher. If mortgage rates return to their 60-year average of 8.8 per cent, the average cost of owning a bungalow would reach 80 per cent of after-tax income.[6] That, however, is a national average; in Vancouver and Toronto, the cost would exceed 100 per cent.

Clearly, something would happen before we reached this point. Families straining to cope with the current mortgage burden would not be able to meet the higher payments: they would be forced to sell and either downsize or rent, creating downward pressure on prices in general. For those counting on their home equity to finance their retirement, this would result in possibly substantial reductions in available funds.

In a worst-case scenario, Canada would experience a housing collapse similar to the one that began in the United States in 2006, and recovery could take 10 years or more. The best-case scenario would be a prolonged period of flat or very slowly increasing house prices. Either way, home ownership will not represent the wealth generator it has been in the past, and the group that will endure the biggest impact will be those Canadians making the transition from employment to retirement.

Capital Markets Will Be Less Helpful in Building Wealth

Despite the financial crisis of 2007–2009, the average annual return for pension funds over the 25-year period ending December 31, 2009, remained a healthy 9.1 per cent, easily outpacing inflation, which averaged just 2.5 per cent during the same period.

Canadians who made regular deposits into an RRSP or other capital accumulation plan during this period, and who were fully invested in stocks and bonds, did very well. Just as falling mortgage rates propelled housing prices upward, falling interest rates enhanced the returns on both stocks and bonds—especially bonds. The average annual return on long-term Canada bonds over the 30-year period ending in 2011 was 11.5 per cent, almost 9 per cent higher than the inflation rate for the same period. As we will see, this stunning performance is highly unlikely to be repeated in the foreseeable future.

We are far more likely to witness a potential average annual return on retirement savings of just 5 to 6 per cent over the next 25 years, and this assumes heavy exposure to equities in an investment portfolio. With interest rates at historic lows, bonds will do especially poorly. The yields on bonds may go sideways for a while but can only go up in the longer term, which means that bond prices can only go down.

This is bad news for RRSP owners who count on growth in their plan to fund their retirement years. To give an idea of the impact on your RRSP balance of the expected lower returns, assume that your salary rose steadily over the past 30 years to the point where you are currently earning $100,000 a year. If you contributed 8 per cent of pay to an RRSP over that period, and earned 11.5 per cent annually on your investments, your balance today would be $643,000. If you earned a return of just 5.75 per cent on your investments over the same period, your RRSP balance today would total just $327,000, or barely half as much. Unfortunately, the future is much more likely to resemble the second scenario than the first.

Actually, it's worse than that. Your retirement income will be lower not only because your account balance will be smaller, but also because your investment returns *after* retirement are likely to remain lower than historical returns. To take an extreme case, assume you planned to withdraw all the investment income earned by your portfolio every year after you retire. If you had an account balance of $643,000 and earned 11.5 per cent, your income would be $74,000. If you had an account balance of $327,000 and earned 5.75 per cent, your income would be just $19,000, barely a quarter as much! Of course, you should never have counted on a return of 11.5 per cent per year forever, but who would have thought interest rates and returns would fall so low?

So it's entirely possible that over the next 30 years, your RRSP will generate only a fraction of the income it would have produced in the past. If your retirement date is looming, this is less of an issue than it might otherwise have been because you should have enjoyed some fairly good returns until now, and would only have investment returns after retirement to worry about. If your retirement is still many years off, your ultimate fate is less certain, but it is very likely that your RRSP will not produce the type of retirement income you hoped for. You may be faced with the choice of saving much more for your retirement starting now or saving at the same rate and retiring later. Given the difficulty of saving when the cost of home ownership is so high, you are more likely to save longer and retire later.

The Demographic Pressures that Encouraged Early Retirement

Half a century ago, the world was markedly different from today, in so many ways. In 1961, only one-third of Canadian women were employed outside the home,[7] a figure that doubled over the next 50 years. The impact of this change on the labour force and on unemployment rates has been enormous. Had the participation rate of women in the workforce remained as it was in 1961, there would be 4 million fewer women employed outside the home today. Along with this phenomenon came the entry into the workforce of Canada's baby boomers. This was a demographic tsunami that began in the late 1960s and didn't let up until the early 1990s. It also added millions more workers than if the post-war baby boom had never happened.

On its own, either event would have been significant. Their combined effect created an unprecedented strain on the workforce that has affected our society for decades. Even with the robust economy of the 1960s, jobs could not be created quickly enough to absorb all of the new workers. It is not surprising, then, to see that unemployment rates more than doubled from the 1950s to the 1990s (see Table 4.1).

Table 4.1: Canada's Unemployment Rate before 2000

	Average Unemployment Rate
1950s	4.2%
1960s	5.1%
1970s	6.8%
1980s	9.4%
1990s	9.6%

This massive surplus in the labour supply was everyone's problem. Certainly the workers themselves were affected by it. There was constant pressure on governments to do something, especially back in an era when voters still thought that governments could directly create jobs. Labour was sensitive to the issue as well, because it wanted to find jobs for new workers but not at the expense of older workers. Fortunately there was a remedy that appealed to everyone, which was to encourage earlier retirement.

Everyone including employers could stand to gain by encouraging workers to retire earlier. For employers, it was a practical expedient that allowed them to hire younger and less expensive workers who were looking for their first jobs. Getting workers to retire earlier required good pension plans. As a result, pension plans flourished in the 1970s and early 1980s in particular. The workers themselves benefitted, as younger workers got jobs and older workers got to retire earlier than they otherwise would have done. The situation was enhanced throughout the 1980s when workers were offered early retirement "windows" which gave employees who met certain age and service conditions better pension benefits, provided they retired within a window of time specified by the employer. The strategy had the co-operation of organized labour, which was eager to find jobs for new workers while ensuring that older workers were well-treated when encountering retirement. In effect, the promotion of relatively early retirement was a policy both management and labour could endorse—a double win.

Then it was the turn for federal and provincial governments to add their incentives. High unemployment rates were a perennial election issue in the 1980s and 1990s and governments looked for ways to be seen to be doing something. At some point the light went on: it was easier to encourage older workers to retire and free up jobs for the unemployed than it was to create brand-new jobs. This sparked a whole range of retirement incentives, including:

- legislation in the mid-1960s to regulate registered pension plans;
- the introduction of Canada/Quebec Pension Plans in 1966;
- the reduction of OAS retirement age to 65, phased in between 1965 and 1969;
- the introduction of the Guaranteed Income Supplement (GIS) in 1967;
- improvements in public sector pension plans to provide generous early retirement benefits;
- the establishment of 60 as the earliest age for pension under C/QPP in 1987; and
- a major increase in RRSP contribution limits in 1991.

Some of these programs would have been introduced in any event, but the demographic pressures created the political will to make them happen sooner.

These measures were popular. Employers, young job-seekers, organized labour, and government all benefitted from encouraging older workers to exit the workforce. The older workers themselves benefitted from hefty incentives to retire earlier than planned. The net result was a long-term trend toward earlier retirement, as shown in Figure 4.1.

Figure 4.1: Average Retirement Age in Canada before 2000

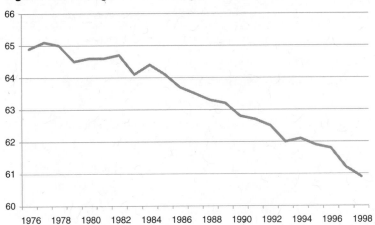

By the early 1990s, all baby boomers had reached working age, and by 2006, female participation in the workforce reached a plateau. By the early 2000s, then, for the first time in 40 years, no new identifiable, large group of people was poised to enter the workforce. The workforce, however, kept growing at a steady rate until the 2009 recession (see Figure 4.2).

Figure 4.2: Total Labour Force (millions)

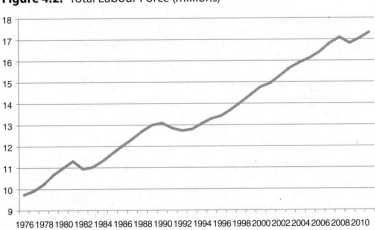

In the period between 1993 and 2008, the labour force grew by a steady 280,000 workers annually. How could this happen when the two forces previously responsible for much of the growth—the maturing of baby boomers and the entry of women workers—were no longer operative? Immigration remained a constant but relatively modest factor, so this could not be the cause.

The new source of labour emerged from the ranks of the unemployed, built up over years of high unemployment and now being tapped. The unemployment rate, as we saw in Table 4.1, more than doubled from the 1950s to the 1990s, topping out in 1993 when it reached 9.6 per cent, which translated into more than 1.6 million unemployed Canadians. In the first decade of this century, the unemployment rate dropped to an average of 7 per cent, which signals a major reversal of a 40-year trend of rising unemployment.

What about the Next 20 Years?

The unemployment rate will continue to decline until we reach the limits of structural unemployment. This is in the vicinity of 5 per cent, similar to the level last seen in the early 1960s, and it will likely take us about 10 years to get there. At that point, we will be in a situation outside the living memory most of the readers of this book, with low unemployment and no large pool of labour to fill the void, with one exception: people in their sixties who have retired or wish to retire and are still capable of working. When this occurs, employers and governments will make an effort to keep people working and keep the economy functioning. Sexagenarians will represent the only group large enough to fill this role.

The labour force is expected to grow by 18 per cent between 2010 and 2040, dramatically lower than the 55 per cent increase experienced in the previous 30 years. In absolute numbers, Canada added about 6.1 million workers to the labour force between 1980 and 2010, yet it is projected to add just 3.1 million in the next 30-year period.

Not surprisingly, the ratio of workers to retirees will change dramatically as well. If we assign everyone between ages 20 and 64 to the working age group, and deem those age 65 and up as retirees, Canada had 6.6 workers for every retiree in 1971. By 2010 the ratio dropped to 4.4, and Statistics Canada's medium growth scenario for the next 25 years indicates just 2.3 workers for every retiree by 2036. That's barely half of today's ratio and a third of the 1971 measure.

The conclusion: Canada will not have enough workers in the years ahead, and various incentives, government policies, and employment practices to encourage early retirement will make little sense. In a reversal of the conditions that presently exist, governments and employers will introduce incentives to encourage later retirement and penalties to discourage early retirement. As a result, Canadians will begin working longer and the average retirement age of 62 will no longer be sustainable.

Putting on our Economist Hats

Let's look at economists' views on what will happen to retirement ages.

In a commentary published by the C.D. Howe Institute,[1] economist Peter Hicks suggested that the average retirement age will rise by about five years between 2010 and 2031, taking it to about age 67. This increase in retirement age would stabilize the producer-to-consumer ratio, which is the ratio of time actually spent at work producing goods and services to time spent not working. The prediction matches our actuarial calculations showing that Canadians would have a much easier time saving for retirement if they continued working a few years longer.

We can't resist making our own rough economic calculation to compare it with the above estimate. The CPP estimated that Canada will add a net 3.1 million people to the labour force over the next 30 years, or about 3 million workers fewer than were added in the last 30 years. This suggests a hefty shortfall, though the extent may be less than 3 million because of productivity improvements and possibly slower economic growth. As a result, the actual shortfall could be closer to 2 million.

Now consider this: if everyone postponed their retirement by four years, raising the average retirement age from 62 to 66, it would add about 2 million people to the workforce by 2040. That is just about the number we need! This simple calculation should be taken with a grain of salt, but it nevertheless suggests a retirement age of 66 or so in the not-too-distant future.

5

When Can We Retire?

In the last chapter, we learned that looming shortages in the labour force will impel governments and employers to take away incentives to retire early. In 20 years' time, the economy will run better if we retire around age 66 or 67 instead of the current average of 62.

You might think: "I'll retire when I can afford to retire, or perhaps a little later when I feel like retiring." This chapter tries to estimate when we can afford to retire about 20 years down the road. We will use actuarial calculations to do this rather than worrying about what is good for the economy. We will consider the question from a national perspective, that is, if everyone saved the same percentage of earnings and retired at the same age, what is that age likely to be in 20 years? It is important to know this because it will be a struggle to swim against the current. If our external environment is going to force the average Canadian to work a lot longer, it will also make it harder for each of us as individuals to retire early.

Even before we start, we know from Chapter 4 that the retirement age is going to be higher than the current average of 62 because demographics and capital markets are starting to work against us. Making a good actuarial estimate for the entire Canadian population is not easy. One complication is that saving currently takes place in all four pillars, as described in Chapter 2. Each pillar entails a different retirement age, a different funding approach, and different survivor benefits. We will simplify our calculations by assuming that all our retirement savings go into one pension plan and that all of our pension will come out of the same plan.

Another complication is that a proper calculation of savings rates requires a sophisticated computer model, because there are so many variables that come into play. For instance, we need to know current demographics, anticipated changes in lifespan, evolving immigration trends, expected labour force participation rates, future unemployment levels, changes in fertility rates, and future inflation. Fortunately, these calculations have already been done for us, since the valuation system used to determine the long-term sustainability of the Canada Pension Plan takes all these variables into account. All we have to do is extend the CPP model to cover the pension from all four pillars, which is a straightforward actuarial exercise.

The third complication is figuring out how to treat lower-income workers. The bottom 40 per cent of workers by income level are not paying the full cost for their retirement now, because they are receiving GIS and they are getting more pension out of OAS than they are contributing in the form of income tax. Our national success in dealing with poverty among the elderly is largely a result of this situation. Since it would be unrealistic—and probably undesirable—to assume this situation will change, we need to modify our calculations to build in a subsidy for lower-income people. In our model, the subsidy would be funded by an extra levy on upper-income groups.

The final issue to resolve before we perform the calculations is determining how much we are saving now for retirement and how much we can realistically expect to save in the future. At a guess, the average reader is probably earning about twice the average national wage. That puts it at $100,000. They are contributing about 2.5 per cent of their total pay toward the C/QPP and another 1 per cent of pay for OAS and GIS through the income tax they pay. They are also contributing anywhere from 0 to 15 per cent toward their employer's pension plan, RRSPs, and TFSAs combined. Their employer is also contributing 2.5 per cent of pay toward the C/QPP and anywhere from 0 to 15 per cent into a pension plan on behalf of the employee. The *median* percentage the employer is contributing into a pension plan is 0 per cent simply because most workers do not have pension plan coverage.

When you put this all together, at least 6 per cent of pay is currently earmarked for retirement in the case of middle-income to upper-middle-income savers, and the total percentage including the employer portion is probably in the range of 12 to 15 per cent. Remember there will be years when the percentage will be very low, such as when one is just starting a new job, or raising a family, or paying off a mortgage. When we factor these low savings years into the average savings rate then even 15 per cent becomes a stretch. Nevertheless, we might save a little more in the future because of new retirement vehicles like Pooled Registered Pension Plans (PRPPs), because the C/QPP might be expanded, and because we will recognize that we don't earn as much as we used to from investments. A reasonable stretch target then is that we can coax or cajole Canadians and their employers to put aside 15 to 20 per cent for retirement purposes in the future. Since we don't have one national plan, this 15 to 20 per cent will go into the C/QPP, toward OAS and GIS in the form of income tax, into RRSPs and TFSAs, and into PRPPs and occupational pension plans.

With this range in mind, we will now calculate the actual savings rates needed to permit retirement at a given age and a given retirement income target. We will do the calculations for retirement ages ranging from 60 to 70. We will also choose two retirement income targets: 50 per cent of final pay and 70 per cent of final pay, though in each case we will set the target higher for lower-income groups, as is described in the sidebar.

The 50 per cent target may seem low but we will discover in later chapters that it is enough to allow most higher-income Canadians to continue their same lifestyle into retirement. Lower-income Canadians will need a higher percentage, which is also reflected in our calculations, even though we will continue to call it the 50 per cent target.

HOW WE CALCULATE THE SAVINGS RATES

The chief actuary of the CPP has determined that the CPP is sustainable over the next 75 years if employers and employees each continue to contribute 4.95 per cent of pay (up to the average national wage) toward the plan. Part of this is to fund past service benefits since there was a time when the CPP was less well funded than today so we are perennially playing catch-up. This part has been ignored so that we reflect only the cost of new benefits being earned. To apply this knowledge to our hypothetical plan that pays the entire pension benefit, we have to convert the CPP benefit into a percentage of final pay, remove the earnings ceiling applicable under the CPP, and then gross up the percentage because the total benefit will be much higher than the CPP benefit alone. We do this at each age between 60 and 70, and then estimate how much more we would need to set aside if the benefit target were 50 per cent or 70 per cent rather than the percentage the CPP actually pays. We then assume that the lowest income quintile doesn't contribute at all and receives a 90 per cent target benefit. We assume the second-lowest quintile contributes only half as much (as a percentage of pay) and receives a 75 per cent target benefit. Because these last two quintiles are paying less, it means the top three quintiles need to pay more to fund that subsidy. This is essentially what happens now through our progressive tax system and is reflected in our calculations.

The 70 per cent target may seem reasonable to a lot of people as most public sector pension plans and some larger private sector plans use the 70 per cent target. But, as we will explain later on, it is in fact higher than most middle- to upper-income households will need. The reasons for this good-news conclusion will become clear in Chapter 10. The main reason for showing the savings rates for the 70 per cent target here is to underscore just how much more expensive it is.

The savings rates needed to reach the 50 and 70 per cent targets are summarized in Table 5.1. These savings rates include whatever savings would be made by the employer on the employee's behalf.

The percentages in Table 5.1 probably look a little daunting. Imagine trying to save 36 per cent of pay every year to reach a 70 per cent

Table 5.1: Saving Rates to Reach Retirement Target

Retirement Age	50% Target	70% Target
60	28%	36%
61	26%	33%
62	24%	30%
63	22%	28%
64	21%	27%
65	20%	25%
66	18%	24%
67	17%	22%
68	17%	21%
69	16%	20%
70	15%	19%

target and retire at age 60! This is totally unrealistic, especially when you consider that the calculations assume the savings rate would be maintained every year from age 25 to retirement. If you started to contribute later on, say at age 35, the savings rate needed to reach the 70 per cent target would have to be more than 50 per cent of pay!

It is safe to assume we are not going to work until age 68 or later on average, at least not in the next 20 years. From our earlier analysis of what Canadians are prepared or able to set aside, it is also safe to assume that the average savings rate will have to be less than 20 per cent of pay if it is to be sustainable, but also more than 15 per cent. This leaves just two possibilities in Table 5.1: that we will retire at 66 or 67, and that we will aim for a 50 per cent retirement income target. Of course, the retirement age and the savings rate may be changed if we aim for an even lower retirement income target. We'll talk more about that in Chapters 11 and 12.

You will note that this actuarial exercise is totally separate from the earlier estimates of when the economy would like us to retire, and yet we still come up with the same result: retirement at 66 or 67. The bottom line is that it will be hard for Canadians to avoid this fate, though individuals can do so through heroic savings efforts or with the help of generous occupational pension plans.

Why Is Retirement So Expensive?

One reason the cost of retirement is so high is that we are living considerably longer than we did even 50 years ago. Over the past century, medical advances and improvements in the quality of life have increased lifespans by nearly 30 years, and there is every indication that this trend is going to continue for the foreseeable future.

The chief actuary for the Canada Pension Plan projects that over the next 70 years, Canadian males who have reached age 65 can expect to live until age 87 versus the current expectation of age 83. For females the news is even better: women who reach 65 can expect to live to 90 years of age. On that basis, men would be spending 25 years of their lives in retirement (assuming an average retirement age of 62) and women would be retired for 28 years. It gets even better: with longer life comes better health over the entire age spectrum. In 1966, 35 per cent of males aged 65 could expect to die within ten years. By the year 2075, the CPP tables indicate only 10 per cent of men that age will die within ten years.

Life expectancy statistics are difficult to apply consistently. Current male life expectancy in Canada may be 78, but reports suggest that a 65-year-old male can expect to live until he's 83. These apparently contradictory statements are both true. The first figure is measured from childbirth and the second from age 65: by the time a man has avoided dying for 65 years, his prospects for a longer life are already very good.

For our purposes, it's important to note that most of the improvement in longevity has taken place at the more advanced ages[1]—in other words, the older you are, the more likely it is that you'll grow even older, within reason. This is significant because it means that new retirees can expect to enjoy more years of retirement than someone of similar age could expect in 1970. For instance, a 65-year-old male in 1970 had only a 25 per cent probability of collecting a pension for 20 years. For a current 65-year-old, that probability has almost doubled—one major reason why pensions have become more expensive.

Why We Won't Save More

So, retirement is expensive, and getting more expensive. We think it will be difficult for Canadians to fully incorporate this reality into their retirement planning. Our spending habits tend to get deeply ingrained and since one has to spend less to save more, it means it is hard to change our saving habits. We can't expect to suddenly adopt a savings rate that is much higher than the rate at which we are saving now. Table 5.2 gives a little insight into why this would be the case. It shows the average annual expenditure for someone with third-quintile earnings (meaning they fall in the middle bracket

Table 5.2: Expenditures for a Typical Working Person[2]

Expenditures	Third Quintile ($)
Food	7,206
Shelter	13,110
Household operation	3,160
Household furnishings	1,573
Clothing	2,350
Transportation	8,645
Health care	1,930
Personal care	1,039
Recreation	3,186
Tobacco and alcohol	1,597
Education	748
Miscellaneous	1,411
Personal taxes	8,517
Personal insurance & pension contributions	3,407
Gifts of money	1,361
Total current consumption	**45,955**
Total expenditure	**59,240**

if earners are divided into five income brackets). When you break expenditures down into categories, it is hard to see how spending could be reduced much in order to make a substantial increase in our savings rates.

Time to Change the Paradigm

A half century ago, Canadians worked nearly five years for every year spent in retirement. Even then, many of our elderly were poor. Today, Canadians work only 1.6 years on average for each year spent in retirement, and they demand a much better lifestyle. It's easy to see that this is not sustainable, especially given the demographic and economic headwinds we are about to face. When many workers exist to support relatively few retirees, no retirement program seems too extravagant. But as the population matures, the cost of unfunded pension programs such as OAS and GIS—and C/QPP before 1997— begin rising as a percentage of GDP.

If we wish to continue retiring at 62, we need to set aside an exorbitant amount of pay to generate a seemingly modest retirement income of 50 per cent of final pay, hence all the stern warnings you have been hearing that we need to save more if we expect to make early retirement attainable. But maybe this is the wrong message. Rather than saving more to retire early, we may be better off saving the same percentage as now and reconciling ourselves to retiring later. Let's face it: that may be the only viable option in any event.

Baby boomers need not worry as much. They can continue to retire fairly early without saving large amounts, especially if they are prepared to use their Pillar 4 assets. The need to lower our expectations (by raising our retirement age) will become more evident about a decade from now, assuming our forecast of lower unemployment rates, slower growth in house prices, longer lifespans, and lower investment returns all come to fruition.

6

How Workers Will Respond

In Chapter 4, we found that the economy will want to keep us working longer in the years to come, simply because we won't have enough younger workers. The best estimate is that the economy's labour needs in 20 years' time would be satisfied if the average retirement age rose from the current 62 to about 66 or 67. Chapter 5 told us that we could, in theory, continue to retire at 62, but it would be increasingly difficult to do so in a world with lower investment returns and longer lifespans, as the real cost of retirement catches up with us. Doing the math, we confirm what we already know: saving for retirement would be much easier if we kept working, at least on a part-time basis, until age 66 or so.

On the surface, then, a convenient win-win situation seems to be emerging. To paraphrase a familiar Buddhist proverb, when the economy is ready to absorb new workers, the workers will appear. That's the theory. But how well is it going to work in practice? Will employees actually be prepared to retire later? There is mounting evidence that both attitudes and actions are evolving rapidly.

A 2008 survey[1] revealed growing acceptance by pre-retirees of at least a moderate increase in the expected age of retirement. The study found that 35 per cent of the respondents aged 45 to 49 who expressed an opinion said they planned to retire after 65. In 1991, only 27 per cent planned to retire after 65. In a 2012 "TD Age of Retirement" report, 17 per cent expected to retire between 66 and 70, and another 11 per cent at 70 or over. These percentages would have been even higher had the survey focused solely on older respondents. It included participants as young as 25; younger people have always expressed a desire to retire exceptionally early, but they tend to change their minds as retirement draws nearer. Looking south of the border, an April 2012 survey conducted by U.S. investment firm T. Rowe Price indicates that a trend to later retirement is already well underway. That survey revealed that 69 per cent of Americans between the ages of 21 and 50 expect to work beyond the traditional age, and three out of four said they would do so because they want to stay active and involved.

Not only are attitudes changing, so are actions. The retirement age in Canada is rising. The watershed year was 1998, when a long-term decline in the average retirement age suddenly reversed direction. Between 1998 and 2012, the average retirement age climbed from just under 61 to a little over 62 (see Figure 6.1).

Figure 6.1: Average Retirement Age Trends

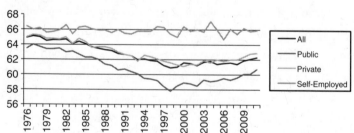

Figure 6.1 is interesting in other respects. It also shows that public sector employees traditionally retire at a younger age than in the private sector. In 1997, the average retirement age in the public sector touched below 58 for the first time. This was made possible by exceptionally generous pension benefits that are payable without reduction as early as age 55 with 30 years of service. Even so, the average age at retirement in the public sector has also been rising. The behaviour of the self-employed is a little curious. They seem to be impervious to any changes in trends as the retirement age for this group has remained steady over the years at about 66.

If a rise from 61 to 62 does not seem that significant, it is because of the way retirement age is calculated. In fact, Canadians are adopting later retirement at a faster pace than the statistics would seem to indicate. The calculation is a weighted average of everyone who reports his or her retirement age, and that average is easily distorted when a disproportionate percentage of the people are younger. Assume, for example, you had 400 people who are 60 years old and another 100 who are 65. If 25 per cent of the people in each of these age groups retire immediately, the average weighted retirement age for that year will be calculated as 61. But in a year's time there will be 300 people remaining who are 61, and 75 more who are 66, so the average retirement age will be higher again. As the bulge of younger people in this example keeps aging, the average retirement age will keep increasing. Because there are so many baby boomers under 60, we can expect to see a more rapid increase in the average retirement age in the years to come.

Since the average retirement age is not the best measure with so many younger boomers, we can turn to the employment rate for a more accurate picture. That is the percentage of people at a given age who are working. For men 55 and over, the employment rate rose from 30.5 per cent to 39.4 per cent over the 13-year period ending in 2010. For women, the rate over the same period almost doubled, going from 15.8 per cent to 28.6 per cent. Figure 6.2 gives more information as to how employment rates have climbed over the long term. It is really since the mid- to late-1990s, when the economy's need for workers started growing, that the employment rates of older Canadians started to rise.

Figure 6.2: Labour Force Trends by Age Group

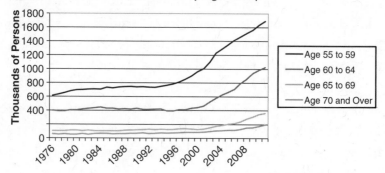

Statistics also show that the average number of years Canadians expect to spend in retirement has stabilized. Until recently, the expected number of years spent in retirement was a growing proportion of total life expectancy; that proportion has been declining in recent years and is now the same as it was in 1977.[2] Maybe we intuitively feel that we shouldn't be spending too great a proportion of our lives in retirement, and while we temporarily moved away from an equilibrium position as our lifespan continued to grow, we are now drifting back to what feels like the right balance.

The Employment Deal Will Need to Change

Large defined benefit pension plans are very telling in terms of how employers feel about older workers. In Canada, such plans often allow for employees to retire with a full pension at an early age. Why do employers offer these early retirement benefits within their plans, especially when starting pensions early is so much more expensive?

There is only one good reason to do so, which is that employers see older employees as not being very cost-effective. If that weren't true, these early retirement incentives would have been eliminated. Too often, workers gradually price themselves out of a job as they approach retirement, especially if they have worked with the same employer for many years. This is just as true in the private sector as it is in the public sector, although private sector employers are usually less generous in the early retirement incentives they offer.

The closer long-term employees come to retirement age, the more the employment deal between the employees and their employers starts to skew in favour of the employees. Long-term employees continue to receive pay increases, extended vacation time, and pensions and other benefits that cost more every year as a percentage of pay. This happens even if productivity fails to keep up with this increasingly expensive compensation package, a situation which anecdotal evidence suggests is common. Because productivity can fall more easily than compensation, older employees tend to be in the driver's seat and the only lever employers can pull is to let these older workers go. Because severance costs are so high for older, long-serving employees, productivity has to fall quite a lot before some employers will finally act.

Some older workers admit that they do not like to work the long hours they put in when they were younger, while others bristle at the suggestion that they are less productive than they used to be. The actions of employers, however, speak for themselves. If employers believed older workers were just as productive, dollar for dollar, as their younger counterparts, they would not offer them hefty severance packages or expensive pension benefits to retire early. In a 2011 study by the Society of Actuaries, 41 per cent of retired workers in the U.S. retired earlier than planned, compared to only 4 per cent who retired later than planned. The early retirees were forced out by employers seeking to cut costs.

It doesn't have to be this way. Employers terminate older workers because it is easier to provide them with generous early retirement incentives and large severance packages than to negotiate new conditions of employment as productivity starts slipping. For the most part, older workers would rather continue to work—albeit with shorter, more flexible hours—than take full retirement. As long as they are healthy, most people want to stay engaged and be useful.

Given the looming labour shortage, employers and employees have to find a way to keep the employment deal fair to both parties as employees cross the 60-year threshold. Employers can offer concessions such as shorter and more flexible working hours. In doing so, employers will still want to ensure that pay is commensurate with productivity, else why bother to offer concessions when they could just hire younger workers? For their part, employees will need to be flexible as well, which means being prepared to accept lower pay and possibly reduced benefits at a certain point in their career, so that their services remain cost-effective.

Accepting reduced compensation goes against the grain of the labour movement, but it is in the best interests of employees to be open to the idea. After all, they are prepared to accept lower pay and lesser benefits now, just not with the same employer. Employees who retire from or lose their regular job will make all sorts of compromises with a subsequent employer to continue working. It doesn't matter if the reason to continue working is that they need the money or just want to stay busy. It will be more efficient if this process of renegotiating the employment deal can happen without a change of employers and, as indicated below, we might be moving in that direction.

Part-Time Work Will Become the Norm for Older Workers

Employees in both Europe and the U.S. seem to be embracing the idea of part-time work in one's final years. As reported in *Benefits and*

Pensions Monitor, a survey by the Netherlands insurer Aegon shows that a growing number of workers have accepted that their retirement will likely be a phased process. It found that, in the U.S. and Europe, more than 60 per cent of respondents anticipate needing part-time jobs after retiring. Only 18 per cent said they planned to stop working immediately after reaching retirement age.

The European study is significant in that it focused on phased retirement. Staying in the workforce longer will be a lot more palatable if one no longer has to work full time. Consider the Vita Needle Company in Needham, Massachusetts, where the median age of employees is 73.[3] The company manufactures needles and tubing for medical, auto, and other sectors, and cultural anthropologist Caitrin Lynch calls the factory an "oasis of meaning for older adults." Their work gives employees a sense of purpose, social interaction, and community identity. The primary attraction for these older workers, however, is flexibility in the hours they work and the tasks they perform. The employees enjoy fitting their work around other parts of their lives, a situation they themselves describe as win-win. Lynch calls it "eldersourcing," and it may represent a significant trend.

Canadians who are 60 and older accounted for one-third of all job gains from July 2009 to the end of 2011, even though they represent only 8 per cent of the workforce, part of a trend that began around 2000. Since that year, the employment rate among older workers has climbed from 13 to 22 per cent. Most of these older workers are taking on non-standard work, meaning part-time or temporary work, and self-employment. Moreover, they are doing so by choice rather than outright necessity, reinforcing anecdotal information that the majority of people over 60 want to remain attached to the workforce, but few want to work full time.

Not everyone who continues working into their sixties does so voluntarily. Some need the money. More workers will fall into this category in about 15 years when the starting age for Old Age Security rises from 65 to 67. Money issues may remain a common problem: about 44 per cent of respondents in one Canadian survey[4] expect to have some debt when they retire, and a majority of them believe it could delay their retirement. Which brings up a rule we cannot stress strongly enough: *never retire with debt!* If you cannot avoid having debt when you want to retire, you have no business retiring.

Will People Save More to Retire Early?

In spite of dire warnings from financial institutions and industry experts either to save more or face poverty, Canadians generally have not changed their habits when it comes to saving for retirement. One recent survey[5] revealed that among Canadians aged 25 to 64 who were asked to name the single most important factor when they considered a job opportunity, only 7 per cent cited good retirement benefits. Salary and flexible work arrangements were deemed far more important. This should not come as a total surprise. It's a basic tenet of human behaviour that dealing with present-day matters is more important to us than planning for events that are still many years off. As they have in the past, Canadians will react to their pension concerns as retirement age draws closer. At that point, the only remedy may be to stay in the workforce longer than they might have wished because they won't be able to ramp up their saving fast enough to afford to retire early.

Even if people do think about retirement planning, little evidence exists that they are prepared to increase their retirement contributions for the privilege of being able to retire early decades down the road. It is true that public sector workers have been doing just that in recent years, but they have no choice. Those who save through RRSPs do have a choice. The median contribution to an RRSP in 2010 was 5.7 per cent of the average national wage, down somewhat from levels in 2006 and 2007, before the international financial crisis reduced account balances in most RRSPs.

In most public sector plans, the responsibility for funding pension benefits is shared. Governments in several jurisdictions recently announced that public sector plans under their sponsorship will require employees to pay half the cost of pensions, which is substantially more in most cases than the share they currently pay. It appears the days of employers writing a blank cheque for retirement costs will soon be over. In some cases, members will be contributing as much as 13 per cent of pay. Once the contribution rate climbs beyond 10 per cent, employees will justifiably balk at paying more, which may make them more amenable to accepting lower benefits instead. This is already happening, with some plans increasing pensions by only half the change in the CPI, rather than 100 per cent of the change, as had been granted in the past. This is yet another sign that people, recognizing that the cost of early retirement is becoming untenable, are beginning to accept the inevitability of receiving lesser, or at least later, pensions instead of contributing more.

A New Measure of Grey Power?

With Canadians living longer and the proportion of seniors growing quickly, we can expect to see at least a subtle shift in their political clout. Politicians will have to pay particular attention to what older workers and seniors want. For example, seniors have been clamouring for changes to Registered Retirement Income Funds (RRIFs) so that they don't have to start withdrawing their money so soon. Currently, RRSP assets must be transferred to a RRIF by age 71, and the amount that has to be withdrawn each year is more than some retirees want to withdraw. They feel the current minimum guidelines are causing their RRIF balance to be drawn down too quickly, especially in the present low-interest environment.

While older Canadians constitute a significant constituency pressing for changes, their sheer number ironically will also limit the extent of change that politicians can engineer on their behalf. How much more can we spend on health care when it already takes up such a large percentage of government spending? And how can more of those healthcare dollars be allocated to seniors when the current share they are receiving is so high? It will be interesting to see how questions like these play out.

7

Deciding When to Retire

Have you ever been out for a late autumn walk in the closing part of the afternoon, and suddenly looked up to realize that the leaves have practically all gone? And the sun has set and the day gone before you knew it—and with that a cold wind blows across the landscape? That's retirement.

—Stephen Leacock

Leacock's bleak perspective on retirement has been shared by other luminaries in the arts and music worlds. Ernest Hemingway observed, "Retirement is the ugliest word in the language." The American comedian George Burns quipped, "Retirement at 65 is ridiculous. When I was 65, I still had pimples." And French writer and philosopher Simone de Beauvoir declared, "Retirement may be looked upon either as a prolonged holiday or as a rejection, a being thrown on to the scrap-heap."

Artists, scientists, and musicians don't care much for that prolonged holiday, and many reject the idea of retirement entirely. Picasso was still painting when he was 90, Einstein pursued the Grand Unified Theory right up to his death at 76, and Pablo Casals practised his cello three hours a day at 93. Now 76, movie director Woody Allen shows no signs of slowing down. And Mick Jagger can't get any satisfaction from contemplating retirement. Show business is filled with senior citizens who refuse to stop working. Visit Las Vegas and you'll find no shortage of septuagenarians who are still milking their hits from the 1960s. This theme extends to the business sphere as well. Billionaire businessman Kirk Kerkorian is still busy making deals at 95, while Donald Trump, the poster boy for American brashness who seems youthful from a business perspective, is 66 and far from done.

Obviously, money is not what keeps these people working. All of them had earned more than enough by the time they were 50 if not younger. They kept on going for other reasons. It's not even about the ability to be creative. That can't be why Wayne Newton sang "Danke Schoen" almost every night for more than 40 years. If it's not about the money and not about doing creative work, then what is it?

The key to why some people stay engaged in the workforce and others want to get out is elusive. Anecdotal evidence, as well as some statistics on the self-employed, suggest that the one primary factor that keeps people working beyond normal retirement age is "owning the experience." Others might use the phrase "having control." Note that self-employed Canadians retire at 66 on average, even though they are generally more affluent than employees, who retire much sooner. For instance, Hart, a 69-year-old we know, continues to put in long days at his furniture business, week after week. Hart doesn't need the money anymore, and selling furniture is not the most creative endeavour, so he is not working because his field is so intrinsically interesting. He is still working because he is the boss, which means he owns the experience, and that is enough to keep him engaged.

Other examples abound. The barber of one of the authors is a friendly guy named Sal. Sal is 68 and has been working at the same location in mid-town Toronto since 1960. When asked whether he plans to retire soon, Sal emphatically shakes his head, no. He reasons that retirement is "the end of the road." Moreover, he would miss talking to clients every day and "solving the problems of the world." He confides with a smile that his ultimate goal is to retire at 95 and get shot by a jealous husband at 96. A little more seriously, he admits that he may slow down in due course to working just a couple of days a week, but why retire fully?

A lawyer friend, David, who is 59 and a partner in a law firm, sees no reason to retire until he's 75 or older. David can control his working environment, including his hours and the cases he chooses to accept. To his way of thinking, why retire outright, if you can simply slow down as you get older? David even has a role model for this way of thinking: an uncle of his, also a lawyer, continues to practise law at 83.

By contrast, people who work for someone else retire at 62, on average. If they had better pensions, they would leave even earlier. That's certainly the case in the public sector, where the average retirement age is closer to 60. People probably wouldn't retire so early if they were motivated by their jobs. Older workers in this situation have little control over what they do or how they do it, a fact that's as true of middle managers in an office setting as it is of assembly-line workers. It is hard to be engaged if you see yourself as a cog in the machinery of a large corporation, with no sense of ownership.

Some employees are pushed out prematurely by employers because the employment deal between employee and employer becomes too heavily skewed in favour of employees as they approach retirement age. As we concluded in Chapter 6, older employees literally price themselves out of their jobs when their vacation entitlement, benefits, and cash compensation grow faster than their productivity at a certain stage in their careers. Illness or family members needing care contribute to the decision to retire early in some cases, but retirement is most often forced by job loss.

It is better that we retire on our own terms rather than getting pushed out. It is also important that we can gain control of our lives upon retirement; otherwise we are simply giving up one unsatisfactory situation to engage in another. We should all do some soul-searching about our motivation to retire, a step too often overlooked by workers and counsellors alike. Retirement planning is focused too much on *how* and not enough on *why*. Even if our work is not as creative as Picasso's or Einstein's, most of us will be happier staying engaged in the workforce, provided we can maintain some control over our lives by negotiating shorter and more flexible hours once we reach 60. This will likely take some initiative on the part of employees to start a dialogue with their employers about reshaping roles and work hours, because employers are unlikely to take the first step. Part of that dialogue, by the way, will require that employees be prepared to be flexible with their compensation and benefits demands. This approach won't succeed in every job situation, but the more often employees try, the sooner it will become the norm. It will also require employers to amend their pension plans to recognize the need for greater flexibility.

This isn't just for our own benefit. It's for the benefit of Canadian society generally. As we have seen, we will have to delay retirement to meet the needs of the economy, yet the vast majority of people approaching retirement age show little interest in working long hours on a regular basis. And employers who speak openly on the matter show little appetite for keeping a large number of 60-somethings around on a full-time basis. Getting older workers to stay longer on a part-time basis seems to be the answer.

The Case for Retiring Early

Not everyone agrees with the idea of extending working years. In response to a column Vettese wrote for the *National Post* newspaper on the virtues of working longer, one reader commented, "I retired at 52 and never looked back. Not once did I miss the office." At least two other readers indicated they agreed with this point of view. And yet it is just as easy to find men and women in Canada who retired early and spent many years regretting their decision because they had lost identity and purpose in life.

Some acquaintances who retired fairly young with generous defined benefit pensions talk about how good life is and how much they are enjoying their retirement. We have to take these claims with a grain of salt. The retirement process is hard to reverse and few people want to admit they made a mistake by leaving too early. Many new retirees will genuinely revel in their newfound freedom, which enables them to do things they had meant to do for years but didn't have the time. That doesn't mean it will work out in the longer run. It brings to mind a statement by former Chinese leader Zhou Enlai who, when asked for his opinion on the significance of the French Revolution of 1789, is said to have replied, "It is too soon to tell." Similarly, individuals who retired a few years earlier may claim they enjoy the total freedom from work, but it may be too soon to tell. One acquaintance who retired a few years ago and who initially enjoyed his retired lifestyle now admits he is looking for a job to keep himself busy. Another who retired five years ago (in his late fifties) and who is still enjoying retirement acknowledges that his wife recently mused out loud, "Is this what we'll be doing for the next 25 years?"

The point is, your decision about when, how, and where to retire is as important, in its own way, as the original career decision you made all those years ago. Choosing a retirement age isn't the same as picking an ice-cream flavour. We're talking about how you will spend your last 20 or 30 years on Earth.

Planning Your Retirement

Now that you have something to think about in terms of your work-life balance during your post-60 years, you still need to decide:

1. when to retire;

2. the living standard you will aim for; and

3. the kind of estate you want to leave your heirs.

Note that these decisions are all tied together. The earlier you retire, the lower your standard of living, either after retirement if you haven't saved enough, or before retirement if you saved heavily. Similarly, a desire to make large bequests to your children may limit the amount you feel you can spend in retirement.

When to Retire

If you are under 55, keep in mind that most of your peers will probably maintain an attachment to the workforce until their mid- to late-sixties, as we discovered in the earlier chapters. That's their decision but, among other concerns in case you plan to retire early, consider how you'll spend your time if many of your friends are still working. They won't have the same opportunity to play golf or travel as you have.

If you are 60 or over and are still enjoying your work, ask yourself why you want to retire. Of course, if you don't enjoy your work, and you have no means of improving your working environment by doing something else or working more flexible hours, then consider what type of living standard you can expect. Your retirement income will grow by about 6 per cent of your final pay for every year that you keep working.

The Living Standard You Will Aim For

A Morneau Shepell survey showed that nearly 100 per cent of respondents say they would be happy to have the same standard of living (or slightly lower) in retirement that they enjoyed while they were still working. You will remember there were times in your life when your expenses were high—paying the mortgage on your first house, making payments on your first car, putting your children through school—and yet you still managed to get by. Imagine how much easier it would have been without those expenses, and you get an idea of what you'll need in retirement. In addition, you may be overestimating how

active you'll be after you retire, or how much you'll spend on recre-
ational activities. For instance, research shows that many pre-retirees
believe they will travel more during retirement than they actually do.
The same goes for expenditures on recreation. Few of us change our
life habits when we retire.

The most important guideline is this: your living standard and
your intended retirement age are closely connected. The later you
retire, the better your living standard will be, assuming you continue
saving for retirement during those extended working years. The earlier you retire, the more you have to save for retirement, which means
the lower your living standard will be during your working years.

Once your income has reached a certain threshold, your happiness in retirement is not tied very closely to your standard of living.
The affluent also have their anxieties. An ambitious study conducted
by Boston College in 2008 makes this point dramatically. The study
surveyed only the super-rich: subjects included in the study had to
possess investable assets of $25 million or more. The 165 households
who responded to the questionnaire had average assets of $78 million.
When asked if they felt financially secure, the average response was
that *they would need about 25 per cent more money than they already had
in order to feel secure.* It seems that excessive wealth over time becomes
more of a burden than a comfort. The type of enjoyment that ordinary people will get from the odd bout of conspicuous consumption,
such as a shopping spree in New York or a trip to Las Vegas, is lost
on the super-rich. Through what psychologists call "habituation," the
psychological benefit of conspicuous consumption vanishes when it
becomes the norm.

What You Plan to Leave Behind

We all share a natural desire to take care of our children, even when
they are no longer children. One of the ways many of us plan to do

this is to pass along a sizeable inheritance, but it's wise to be clear about your intentions. Your children may still be school age as you read this, but by the time you die, they may well be on the verge of retirement themselves. If your children are successful in their jobs, they may need money from you only three times in their lives: to complete their schooling; to start their own business; and to help purchase their first house. Beyond these needs, you may be better off spending your money on yourself. Do you really want your children to remain close to you only because of the size of your bank account and the promise of a large inheritance? Have you read *King Lear* recently?

Perhaps a good middle-of-the-road approach is to *hope* that you can pass along a sizeable inheritance to your children, but to live as if such a bequest isn't important if it fails to materialize. As we note in the next chapter, if you can make it through Phase 1 of your retirement, you are more likely to under-spend than overspend in Phase 2, so you will probably have more assets at the point of death than you expected. If you don't, you should feel satisfied that you have already done your duty for your children.

It's All a Balancing Act

The most valuable insight we glean from these findings is that happiness really isn't about money. Once you have enough income to pay for the necessities of life plus the odd indulgence, the incremental benefit of more money is minimal. Family, friends, identity, achievements, and experiences are all more important.

If it's still important to be very comfortable in retirement, and reaching that level requires you to make substantial sacrifices during your working years to accomplish it, ask yourself why it is such a high priority after retirement, but not before. The best reason to postpone retirement is because you are enjoying the work-life balance achieved late in your career more than you would enjoy total retirement. The key word is *balance*. Spending every penny during your working years and reaching an age when you are unemployable is obviously a bad idea. Saving every penny and living a grim existence during your working years so that you can enjoy a lavish lifestyle in retirement isn't much better. And what if you become afflicted with ill health early in your retirement and never get a chance to enjoy the money you were saving all those years?

Retirement and Debt

It may seem unnecessary to say it again, but you should almost never retire while you still have debt. Yet, as we saw in Chapter 6, a considerable percentage of Canadians expect to do just that. If you are relying on savings accumulated during your working years, a substantial part of those savings should be invested in bonds or other fixed-income investments; no retiree should have 100 per cent of their assets in equities, because they can't risk the impact of a major market crash on their savings. This is why having debt makes no sense. If you hold fixed-income investments to generate income, and make interest payments on debt at the same time, the interest you are paying on your debts will always exceed the interest you are earning from your investments.

There are just two situations in which you might be justified carrying some debt into retirement. One is where you have a large defined benefit pension from which you continue to make payments toward liquidating your debt for a fixed period of time until the debt is erased. The other is when you expect to pay off the debt within a few years of retirement, and you would incur a hefty penalty by paying it off early. Even in these situations, the goal is to be totally debt-free as soon as possible.

8

The Three Phases of Retirement

Most advice on how much one needs to save seems to rest on a rather one-dimensional view of retirement. When most of us contemplate retirement, we picture ourselves more or less as we are now, just a little older and greyer, and maybe a little stiffer, but otherwise the same. In retirement, we are still up for that exotic trip, a night out on the town, or a golf game. That may very well be true, but only in the first phase of retirement. We don't like to think about it, but we will likely go through phases when we will be less healthy. By one estimate,[1] the disability-free life expectancy of Canadians is 68.6 years, meaning we could have more than a decade of retired life when we will have to cope with health issues.

A Society of Actuaries survey of Americans in the pre-retirement stage shows that about 30 per cent do little or no retirement planning. Of those who do, nearly two out of three focus their planning only on Phase 1 of retirement. As we will see below, they are likely to overstate their financial needs in their later retirement years. You need to know what to expect in all phases of retirement and build that knowledge into your retirement planning.

Phase 1

Not surprisingly, Phase 1 is the most active phase of retirement and probably very much the way you pictured retirement, assuming you are fortunate enough to avoid serious health issues. During this phase, your physical and mental abilities will be similar to what they were just before retirement, although you might have lost a few yards off your golf drive and you might find it easier to get one of your grown children to set up Skype on your laptop rather than do it yourself. In Phase 1, there is a good chance you will engage in part-time paid work or some volunteering.

Phase 1 is the time to pursue any goals you didn't have time for during your regular career. Travelling to exotic locations and taking up a new hobby are common Phase 1 activities. You will also be physically active and might even be in better shape than you were in your last few working years. The duration of this phase varies considerably, but it typically stretches from retirement age to your mid- to late-seventies; it can extend into your eighties if you are blessed with good genes and take care of yourself.

Phase 2

Unfortunately, Phase 1 does not last forever, at least not for most people. At some point, you will find you have entered the second phase of retirement, in which your physical and/or mental capacity will be significantly diminished. You will be travelling less, if at all, and you will have cut back on other strenuous activities. It is unlikely you will be still working during Phase 2. For some, the transition is so gradual that they couldn't tell you when they crossed over into Phase 2. For others, the change might be precipitated by the onset of a serious illness or a stressful event, such as the death of a spouse.

As we describe later in this chapter, there is a good chance that consumption will decrease during Phase 2, simply because one has less opportunity or ability to consume. The type of changes that might cause consumption to rise do not usually happen until the last phase.

Phase 3

If you enter Phase 3 of retirement, it means you are physically or mentally impaired, which will severely curtail your range of activities, probably for the rest of your life. You will need to be in a nursing home at this stage, or if you are wealthy enough, you might opt for home care or an upscale retirement home supplemented with private nursing assistance.

Spending in Phase 2 and Phase 3

A widely held belief is that pensions need to be fully protected against inflation. For those who have come to this conclusion using rational analysis, this belief stems from the premise that retirement is all about Phase 1, but, as we have just seen, it is more complicated than that. Given that one's lifestyle will be so fundamentally different in Phase 2 and Phase 3, it is not surprising that spending habits and overall consumption will change as well.

Most of us already have a hunch that consumption declines with advanced age. If you had a middle-class upbringing, you might have had a grandmother who gave cash gifts to her grandchildren every so often because she no longer spent the money on herself. She probably had neither bought a car nor travelled anywhere for years. Once people enter their eighties, they just seem to be less inclined to spend money. But we can't rely on anecdotal evidence for something this important. Fortunately some hard data exists.

A 1992 German study[2] is particularly useful. Based on a detailed survey of over 40,000 households headed by a senior, it found that the actual spending behaviour of retirees is very different from what theory predicts. Wealth should be declining with age as one draws down one's assets and that does in fact happen until about age 70, but then, rather unexpectedly, wealth starts increasing again. This happens because older retirees save more than younger retirees. They even save more than people who are still working!

The rate at which someone saves is a better indicator of income adequacy than the rate at which they spend. If older retirees are spending less, one might suppose it is because they have less to spend. If they are saving more, however, then we have to look elsewhere for a reason. Germans aged 50 to 54 save a little more than 6 per cent of their net income. As we would expect, this savings rate falls after retirement and drops to as low as 2.3 per cent at 65. After that, however, the savings rate starts increasing steadily until it reaches 10 per cent for persons 80 or older.

There are several ways we can try to explain this phenomenon. One is that it is a statistical aberration caused by a small percentage of wealthy older retirees who are skewing the results while the less wealthy majority are spending every penny. This interpretation can be ruled out for two reasons. First, the wealthiest 2 per cent of households were left out of the study. Second, further investigation showed there was little difference between the average savings rate and the median in this case. Another possible explanation is that older retirees are saving extra in contemplation of their own mortality: they wish to leave a large bequest to their children. This possibility can also be ruled out. The researchers found no significant difference between the savings rates of retirees with children and those without children.

Perhaps once they reach age 70, retirees start to worry more about the health expenses they are going to incur at an advanced age and save more in anticipation of that development? This explanation is not very compelling: in Germany, as in Canada, almost all major healthcare costs are covered under a mandatory public system. The only exclusions are self-medication, home care, and prolonged stays in higher-end old-age homes.

It appears the primary reason for saving more is that the very elderly have fewer opportunities to spend. Health can deteriorate, which inhibits travelling, or even driving a car. The death of a spouse or close friends can increase isolation and make it difficult (or just not as interesting) to spend money on entertainment. And why buy a new sofa when the existing one works perfectly well? Indeed, a breakdown of expenditures by age shows that while spending per capita on health rises modestly with age, spending on transportation, travel, clothing, and durable goods drops dramatically.

But maybe Europeans are different from North Americans? To test this, we turn to a large U.S. study published recently by the Employee Benefit Research Institute (EBRI). With spending at age 65 as the benchmark, the study found that household spending fell by 19 per cent by age 75 (which is around the start of Phase 2), 34 per cent by age 85 (roughly the end of Phase 2), and 52 per cent by age 95 (well into Phase 3). As stunning as these figures are, the drop could have been even steeper if older Americans didn't spend so much on health care. Healthcare expenditures after 65 in the U.S. are higher than in Canada or Germany.

What About Canadian Retirees?

So, Germans spend less than they could in their later retirement years. The very elderly in the U.S. also get by on much less. What about Canadians? The underlying situation is similar in many respects among the three countries. Per capita incomes are comparable. Government pensions are reasonably good and are indexed to inflation after retirement. The average retirement age is in the low six-ties in all three countries. Finally, most healthcare costs are covered by the state, although less so in the U.S. Keeping this information in mind, it is not surprising that spending patterns in Canada are not very different from those in Germany or the U.S.

A 1997 survey by Statistics Canada gives details of the sources and uses of income by age group for fully retired senior couples. This data is not readily accessible but that didn't stop well-known actuary Malcolm Hamilton from unearthing the facts. In a paper on the subject,[3] Hamilton reported that older retirees either saved or gave away a substantial amount of their income on a regular basis. The households where the head is 85 or older set aside a whopping 18.6 per cent of their net income in the form of savings or gifts. This is the result for the average Canadian household, not the wealthy, for whom the savings rates would presumably have been even higher. In other words, very elderly people with average incomes in Canada are not even close to spending all their income.

As we have seen, all our government pension programs in Pillars 1 and 2—the Old Age Security pension, the Guaranteed Income Supplement, and the Canada/Quebec Pension Plan—are fully indexed to inflation. Most public sector plans are fully indexed as well. Since these sources make up a significant portion of overall income for the average retiree, the various studies all point to the same conclusion: retirement income derived from RRSPs does not have to increase annually to cover inflation, at least not after age 70 or so. You might still want to buy an annuity at retirement with the proceeds from your RRSP, but there is little or no reason to buy an indexed annuity.

As we will see elsewhere in this book, most people don't buy annuities. At retirement, they transfer their RRSP balance into a Registered Retirement Income Fund (RRIF), and then draw an income from the RRIF every year for the rest of their lives. There are tax rules governing the minimum and the maximum amounts one can withdraw each year. The most common complaint made by retirees is that the minimum amount they must withdraw is more than they are comfortable about withdrawing. They are afraid they will deplete their RRIF account and have little left if they live until their nineties. In fact, they should be more afraid of the opposite, of not withdrawing enough, and having a significant unspent amount remaining in their RRIF when they die. Given their likely spending habits in Phases 2 and 3, most retirees can probably draw greater income from their RRIFs in the early years of their retirement than they now do, without jeopardizing their financial situation later on.

9

We Are Better Prepared than We Thought

Based on what we discovered in the first two chapters, we can be confident that we will avoid outright poverty in our retirement years. Even if we don't save diligently, Canada's social safety net will ensure that we still have a roof over our heads and food on the table. This is a good thing, of course, but is that all we expect? Of course not! We want to keep on living a full life after we retire and part of this involves maintaining the same standard of living we had when we were working. To do so will take money.

By all appearances, Canadians are not preparing adequately for their retirement. Former Bank of Canada Governor David Dodge said as much when he asserted that, "except for the working poor, Canadians must save a very high fraction of pre-retirement earnings every year . . . to provide for reasonably adequate and assured retirement incomes."[1] Clearly this hasn't been happening. Three quarters of private sector workers will retire without a workplace pension, while barely a third of taxpayers contribute to an RRSP in any given year. It sounds as though many of us will be suffering a dramatic drop in our standard of living after retirement, but is this true?

It is easier to answer this question if we first break it down into smaller pieces. Since the answer depends on income level, the first step is to divide up all households into five equal-sized groups, known as quintiles. Each quintile holds 20 per cent of Canadian households and the average income within each quintile is successively higher than the previous one. Table 9.1 shows the breakdown for households consisting of two persons or more. For instance, the average household income in Quintile 4 is $110,000. In Quintile 5, which represents the highest 20 per cent of households, the average is $204,000.

Table 9.1: Population Breakdown by Income Group[2]

Income Quintile	Average Total Income
Quintile 1 (lowest)	$29,000
Quintile 2	$53,000
Quintile 3	$78,000
Quintile 4	$110,000
Quintile 5 (highest)	$204,000

The average income in each quintile might seem high but remember that this is for households consisting of two or more persons; in many cases there are two income-earners.

Now that we have our breakdown, we can decide to ignore the top 20 per cent of households (Quintile 5) as well as the bottom 20 per cent (Quintile 1). For the most part, the people in Quintile 5 will have homes and retirement assets in the form of RRSPs or workplace pensions. They will also have accumulated other assets, such as second homes and investment portfolios. Of course, they can still benefit from some preparation for retirement, and in a later chapter we will consider their retirement planning needs in some detail. We just don't have to worry about them here. We can also ignore Quintile 1 because the government takes care of them through various programs. They will have more after-tax income in retirement than they had while they were working.

That leaves the middle-income earners, the giant swath of 60 per cent of all Canadian households represented by Quintiles 2, 3, and 4. No doubt they want the same standard of living after retirement that they enjoyed before, which is to say, they want to maintain their consumption level. We define consumption to include all discretionary spending, excluding what we set aside as retirement saving or for investment purposes, such as mortgage payments on our home or a second property.

This brings us to a very important point. Consumption is a better measure of affluence than income, since income is only worth something if you can spend it. An income of $50,000 after retirement might allow you to consume as much as $100,000 of employment income because the latter comes with strings attached, in the form of higher taxes, mortgage payments, and retirement saving, all of which reduce your discretionary consumption.

Most middle-income earners naturally aim to achieve in retirement a consumption replacement rate of 100 per cent. That is to say, they expect to consume at the same level after retirement as they did before, so that the ratio of spending before and after remains constant. Spending, for the purposes of this calculation, excludes monies set aside for saving or investment or monies spent on others (children in particular). It is important to keep in mind that the retirement income that is needed to achieve a 100 per cent consumption replacement rate is a lot lower than 100 per cent of the income we had before retirement. This is a key fact because it gives us a glimmer of hope that we may not fare too badly in retirement in spite of a drop in income.

The other important fact that makes our consumption goal in retirement attainable is that we have more sources of wealth than we realize. Most retirement projections fail to take into account the Pillar 4 assets we described in Chapter 2. These are assets that we hold outside of tax-sheltered vehicles including real estate and equity in a business. It turns out that Pillar 4 assets amount to a staggering sum. Calculated during the fourth quarter of 2009, Table 9.2 shows the aggregate assets (net of liabilities) held by Canadians.[3]

Table 9.2: Aggregate Assets Held by Canadians

Category	(in billions)
Pension assets including RRSPs, workplace pension plans and C/QPP investments (Pillars 1, 2, and 3)	$1,860
Real estate equity, net of mortgages (Pillar 4)	$1,917
Other financial and non-financial assets (Pillar 4)	$2,619
Less consumer debt (Pillar 4)	($536)
Net worth	**$5,859**

The most startling statistic in this table is the amount held in "other financial and non-financial assets," a figure totalling more than $2.6 trillion. Even though this is only part of Pillar 4, the category dwarfs pension assets by almost $750 billion!

To a large extent, middle-income Canadians own much of the country's Pillar 4 assets. Evidence that this is the case can be found in "Financial Facelift," the column by Dianne Maley that appears weekly in the *Globe and Mail*. "Financial Facelift" focuses on working-age people (usually couples, but not always) who are seeking advice to help them meet their retirement objectives. According to Maley, the people seeking advice come to the paper of their own volition. The vast majority are middle-income households. They are by no means the wealthiest (who would usually have personal financial advisors) nor are they poor. The one characteristic they have in common is that they care enough to seek advice, meaning they are not much different from the readers of this book!

We collected details from Maley's column over the period from late 2009 to early 2012 and summarized information on 81 cases over that period—usually couples but also some single people—where the primary earner was between 45 and 65. We omitted younger people, because they would not have had time to accumulate significant retirement savings or other assets, and we also omitted the few cases where the head of the household was over 65, because they would likely not be representative of most savers. Table 9.3 summarizes our findings.

Table 9.3: Financial Facelift Summary, 2009–Early 2012

Total Number of Households in the Dataset	81
Number of couples (versus single people)	75
Number owning homes, with positive equity	73
Number with financial assets other than the principal residence or retirement assets	72
Median household income (rounded)	$82,000
Average household income (rounded)	$95,000
Median amount of other financial assets, all cases combined	$119,000
Median amount of other financial assets in cases where the primary earner is age 55 to 65	$161,000

Table 9.3 holds a wealth of information. First, the vast majority are in Quintiles 3 or 4, meaning these are households with income

near the Canadian average, or a little above average. Averages can sometimes be skewed upwards by the presence of a few wealthy outliers, while medians are more representative of the majority of members in a group. In this case, we can be confident that the group is more or less homogeneous since the median household income is not much different from the average. By the way, the fact that 90 per cent of the families in this group own their own home strengthens the case that they are a good representation of middle-income households in the general population.

Even more interesting is that 90 per cent of them have financial assets other than their principal residence or their RRSP. The median value of these other assets is $119,000. These are assets, net of liabilities and mortgage debt. Pillar 4 assets like these go a longer way in retirement than tax-sheltered assets, because income tax has already been paid so these amounts can produce higher after-tax income than is the case for RRSP assets. This means we need to gross up Pillar 4 assets when we add them to RRSP assets in trying to figure out how much retirement income we can generate.

The story gets better. The $119,000 figure was for the entire group aged 45 to 65. Of course, no one expects their asset accumulation to peak at 45, because the best saving years come later, when real earnings are maximized, the mortgage is paid, and child-related expenses start to diminish. If we isolate just the people who are 55 to 65 we find the median assets are $161,000. If we gross this figure up to recognize that tax has already been paid, and then compare it to the retirement savings for the same group, we find the total assets they have at their disposal in retirement are boosted by 67 per cent compared to their RRSP and pension assets alone.

We can conclude that the "Financial Facelift" crowd is better prepared for retirement than they seemed if we considered just their RRSPs and pensions. They can certainly use some of their Pillar 4 assets in their retirement to generate additional income. While this is comforting, it still leaves two questions unanswered. First, is the "Financial Facelift" crowd truly representative of middle Canada? Second, can we quantify their consumption replacement ratios in their retirement years to verify they will do okay? Statistics Canada has the tools to answer these questions for us.

Introducing LifePaths

Besides keeping statistics to track where we are, Statistics Canada also makes projections about what is likely to happen. Over the course of many years, Statistics Canada has developed a sophisticated simulation model called LifePaths to predict outcomes for the Canadian population. LifePaths simulates the behaviour of individuals and families over time with impressive attention to detail concerning their consumption patterns, income, and savings. When you add up all of these individual simulations, it provides a picture of how the country as a whole is doing, and what it will do in the future. As a reality check, the aggregate results from LifePaths are compared against actual statistics on the Canadian population and trued up as necessary.

LifePaths tells us our current state of preparation for retirement, and where we are likely to be in the decades ahead. One chart produced by LifePaths compares expected retirement consumption to actual pre-retirement consumption for the country as a whole. It can show us what proportion of households can expect to see a substantial decline in the standard of living in retirement. Before we get to that chart we need a little more background information.

While we have already established that our target consumption replacement ratio is 100 per cent, Statistics Canada deems that a ratio of 75 per cent is sufficient to provide at least a decent standard of living in retirement in the case of middle- and higher-income Canadians. The 75 per cent threshold is a little arbitrary, but it is probably reasonable when one considers the various dips in our disposable income that we have to endure during the course of our working lives. For instance, the average cost of home ownership in this country is more than 40 per cent of pre-tax household income, which translates into more than 50 per cent on an after-tax basis. If the average homeowner can earmark as much as 50 per cent of net income toward home ownership and still find ways to make ends meet, then a consumption replacement ratio of 75 per cent does not seem so bad. Make no mistake—we still want to reach 100 per cent or close to it, but we can rest easy knowing that anything north of 75 per cent is at least acceptable.

Now that we have established our framework, we can take a hard look at the results of the LifePaths simulation. The original results presented in 2011 by Statistics Canada showed that 13.5 per cent of Canadians who retired in the years from 2006 to 2010 would have consumption replacement rates below 75 per cent. We can call this the "problem group."

At 13.5 per cent, it seems that we should be concerned about the size of the problem group, and indeed that is how the result was originally communicated in press releases and academic papers. The problem group is not as big as it seems, however, when we factor in two critical pieces of data. First, the problem group includes a disproportionate number of the highest-income Canadians (Quintile 5), who have significant resources and are not going to suffer in retirement under any scenario. Second, and equally important, the consumption-replacement rates that were crunched by the LifePaths model didn't take into account the income that can be generated from Pillar 4 assets. As we have seen, these assets are significant. The people at Statistics Canada who run LifePaths acknowledge the omission and say that the model is being updated to take Pillar 4 assets into account.

Rather than wait for Statistics Canada to update their model, we have made an attempt to approximate the result ourselves, using data from various sources. We took the original LifePaths results as our starting point, and then backed out Quintile 1 and Quintile 5 data so that we can focus on the middle-income households. We then added in the approximate income that these middle-income households can generate from their Pillar 4 assets. The adjusted results are shown graphically in Figure 9.1.

Figure 9.1: Consumption Replacement Rates Including Pillar 4 Assets

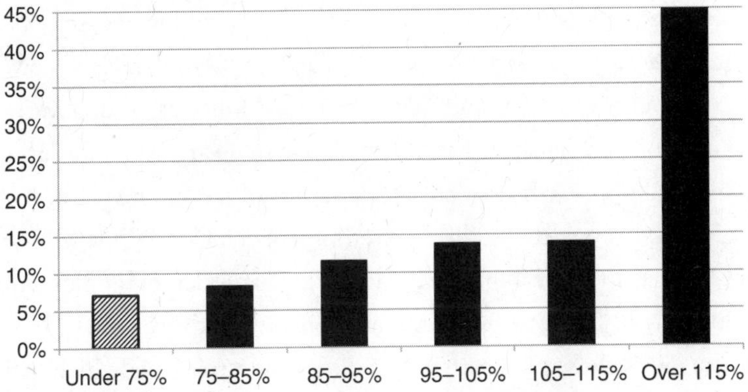

It is hard to overstate the significance of Figure 9.1. First, the problem group (as represented by the striped bar) has shrunk to just 7 per cent of middle-income households versus the 13.5 per cent of all households as computed by Statistics Canada. Second, a whopping 45 per cent of households will have consumption replacement ratios in excess of 115 per cent. That's right—they can spend 15 per cent more in retirement than when they were working. Throw in the group with consumption replacement ratios of 105 to 115 per cent and nearly 60 per cent of middle-income Canadian households will be better off after retirement than when they were working! This is in addition to virtually everyone in Quintile 1. Apart from our estimate of the incremental retirement income due to Pillar 4 assets, we wish to stress that the calculations were performed by Statistics Canada, not by the authors of this book.

No question, the 7 per cent of middle-income households who still remain in the problem group are going to struggle if they try to retire early, but that problem is self-inflicted. Like the grasshopper in Aesop's fable, they chose to spend rather than save. Do we really need to sound the alarm about a national retirement crisis for a group this small? The other 93 per cent of middle-income households will do just fine. In typical Canadian fashion, the glass is nine-tenths full yet we have chosen to characterize it as one-tenth empty.

Some readers will remain skeptical. How could we possibly be doing so well when coverage in workplace pension plans is so low? The answer is rather simple. We have a good foundation of government-sponsored pensions, a favourable tax system, and a lot more ants than grasshoppers who save through a variety of means and not necessarily just through the traditional retirement vehicles. While we saw in Chapter 4 that changing capital markets and demographics will probably translate into lower retirement income in the not-too-distant future, our saving grace is that we will start to retire later, which will offset the fall in retirement income we would otherwise face.

10

Your Retirement Income Target—Why You Don't Need 70 Per Cent

If you're like most Canadians, you are probably tired of hearing you are not saving enough for retirement. For middle-income earners, the challenge of juggling current expenses is difficult enough without worrying about what will happen to you decades from now. Now that you know you are better prepared for retirement than you thought, it won't come as much of a surprise that your retirement income target is almost certainly lower than you have been led to believe. This is not because you should accept a lower standard of living in retirement (you shouldn't). And it's not because your investments will magically perform better in the future than they have over the past decade. In fact, as we noted in Chapter 4, they will probably perform a little worse. No, your real income target will be lower than what you have been told because you have been living off a smaller proportion of your income than you think.

Retirement income targets are usually expressed as a percentage of your household income, before tax, in the final year of employment. The percentage you hear cited most frequently is 70 per cent of your pre-tax income in your last year of full-time employment. On that basis, if your total household income (including that of your spouse) in your final year of full employment was $100,000, you would need to generate $70,000 in annual retirement income from the traditional three pillars: Old Age Security, the Canada/Quebec Pension Plan, and any workplace pension and RRSPs that you accumulated during your working life. For lower-income households, the Guaranteed Income Supplement (GIS) might also play a part. But is 70 per cent realistic or even attainable? Not likely.

Why 70 Per Cent Is Wrong

If 70 per cent were truly your target, you may as well give up. Unless you are in a public sector pension plan, or one of a handful of large, private sector, defined benefit plans, it is almost impossible to achieve 70 per cent by using RRSPs exclusively. Fortunately, 70 per cent isn't close to being a rational target if you are a typical mid- to high-income earner with a family. To understand why your target should be lower, let's reconstruct how 70 per cent came to be commonly accepted.

First of all, certain payroll deductions, such as for CPP and EI, vanish after retirement. Second, we no longer need to keep saving for retirement once we are retired. Third, we will pay less income tax in retirement for a given level of income thanks to the age credit that applies to people over 65, and the pension credit that applies to anyone receiving retirement income, regardless of age. Also, retirees can split their income between spouses and transfer tax credits to the spouse who can best make use of it. Once we make adjustments for these factors, we arrive at a retirement income target in the vicinity of 70 per cent in the case of someone with a middle to upper-middle level of income.

Specific Pre-Retirement Expenditures

This explains how one arrives at a 70 per cent target, but that doesn't make it right. We still need to deduct certain other expenditures that one typically incurs only in the pre-retirement period. We have already mentioned payroll deductions and retirement saving. There are three others: mortgage payments, and child-raising and employment-related expenses.

Mortgage Payments

Certain costs of home ownership, such as insurance, regular maintenance, and realty taxes, carry on for a lifetime. Mortgage payments are different. Most households with middle to high incomes will have to make mortgage payments toward their principal residence for a large part of their working lives, and most will have paid off the mortgage by retirement. While mortgage payments are an unpleasant but necessary outlay, they definitely are not part of your regular ongoing consumption. You should not need to have income to continue making mortgage payments after retirement because the mortgage should be paid off by then.

Child-Raising Expenses

Raising children is expensive and continues for a long time. We will try to quantify it later on in this chapter. Academics usually consider these costs to last until the children reach 18 years of age; clearly, these academics don't have children. While child-related expenses may last until the children are well into their twenties, they should disappear, or at least become infrequent, by that time. The point is, you should not have to worry about having enough income to support children during your retirement years.

Employment-Related Expenses

Certainly, payroll deductions for C/QPP and EI are related to the working phase of your life and will disappear at retirement. In addition, you will have had other expenses that arise because of work. For instance, commuting to work by automobile is an expensive process involving depreciation, insurance, fuel, maintenance, parking, toll roads, and other costs. Commuting by public transit can also add up. Working may also involve business attire, dry cleaning, meals at work, and professional or union dues. These, too, can add up to a substantial amount each year. Once again, you don't need income in retirement to pay for these expenses because you will no longer incur them.

Once all those specific pre-retirement expenditures are eliminated, you are left with only regular ongoing consumption, meaning the sum total of all other expenses you incur in order to live. Statistics Canada categorizes the following items in defining ongoing consumption:

- food
- household operation
- household furnishings
- clothing
- transportation
- health care
- personal care
- recreation (including travel)
- tobacco and alcohol
- education
- personal taxes
- gifts of money

One could argue that regular ongoing consumption actually drops at the point of retirement since retirees can get seniors' discounts and have more time to do certain things themselves, such as preparing meals and gardening. We will be conservative and assume that regular ongoing consumption does not drop in retirement. Since specific pre-retirement expenditures should end by retirement if not before, you should need income only to take care of your regular consumption after retirement. We now have more than an inkling of how your retirement income can be less than 70 per cent of gross income and still be enough to maintain a constant lifestyle. To see how much less, we will start with a simple example.

A Revealing Look at Pre-Retirement Expenditures

For Canadian households in the top two income quintiles where the head of the house is within 10 years of retirement age, at least 90 per cent own their home.[1] The average income level in these two quintiles was shown in Table 9.1. While many are still making mortgage payments, most people will have their mortgages paid off by retirement age.

The average cost of owning a bungalow in Canada over the three years ending 2011 hovered between 40 and 45 per cent of pre-tax household income. Typically about 80 per cent of this cost is due to mortgage payments, but it also includes maintenance and insurance costs. The 40 per cent estimate assumes a 25 per cent down payment on the home, which is more than many buyers can actually make, so the 40 to 45 per cent estimate may be an understatement. The cost is higher for a two-storey home, and higher again for a home in Toronto or Vancouver, where the average cost for a two-storey home recently topped 80 per cent of pre-tax household income!

The high cost of home ownership is not a new phenomenon. It has been high since the 1980s due to either high house prices or high interest rates. For a brief but uncomfortable period in the 1980s, both house prices and interest rates were high simultaneously. Taking a conservative view, let's assume mortgage payments equal 25 per cent of pre-tax income over a period of 25 years before retirement.

For most parents, child-raising expenses are incurred almost exclusively before retirement. The cost is steep. According to a study by People Patterns Consulting,[2] annual child-raising costs for the first 18 years of life amount to $12,800 per child on average (in 2011 dollars) for a two-child household. This doesn't include daycare, which can cost between $600 and $2,000 a month for each child. Even when the child is older than 18, parents usually bear much of the cost of college or university tuition and expenses, along with routine continuing support. Among households with higher income levels, the expense of private schools, summer camps, vacations, specialized (and more expensive) sports equipment, and perhaps lessons in art and music will escalate these costs dramatically. As noted in Table 9.1, the average total annual income for households in the second highest quintile[3] is $110,000; applying the $12,800 average cost mentioned above establishes the cost per child at 11.6 per cent of income. Once again, we will be conservative in our calculation of pre-retirement expenditures and assume child-raising costs of 10 per cent of household income per child, incurred for 21 years.

It also costs money to earn money during full-time employment. Again, we'll be conservative and assume employment-related expenses total 3 per cent of pay, plus employment insurance premiums.

Where does this leave us when it comes to saving for retirement? For now, we will assume that 6.5 per cent of income is contributed into an RRSP by each spouse annually from age 30 until retirement. This is a little more than the Canadian average but less than what some experts think we should contribute. And let's not forget income tax, which we classify as part of regular consumption rather than a pre-retirement expenditure. Fortunately, for the reasons given earlier, the tax bill for a given level of income is less onerous after retirement.

Comparing Pre- and Post-Retirement Expenses

How does this all add up for a typical Canadian household? Assume the household consists of two spouses with employment income and two school-age children. We will assume their total household income is $78,000 which, as we saw from Table 9.1, is very close to the Canadian average for a two-earner household.

If our couple saved 6.5 per cent annually in an RRSP over 35 years, and combine the income their RRSP generates (after being converted to a RRIF at 65) with the pension they can expect from OAS, GIS, and CPP, we estimate their annual retirement income at $48,600, fully indexed to inflation after retirement. (See our assumptions in Appendix C.) This equals "only" 62 per cent of pre-retirement income but, as Table 10.1 shows, it is more than enough to allow the now-retired couple to escalate their regular consumption in rather dramatic fashion.

Table 10.1: Couple with House and Two Children, Average Third-Quintile Income

Retirement at Age 65—All Amounts Rounded	Before Retirement	After Retirement
Total annual income before taxes	$78,000	$48,600
Less RRSP contributions (6.5% of pay)	($5,100)	0
Less CPP contributions	($3,500)	0
Less child-raising costs	($9,400)	0
Less mortgage payments	($13,900)	0
Less employment expenses including EI premiums	($3,700)	0
Less income tax and provincial health premium	($9,600)	($1,700)
Income available for regular consumption	**$32,800**	**$46,900**

This type of before-and-after comparison can be startling the first time you see it. It is hard to believe one can get by with retirement income that is so much less than one's employment income. Even though retirement income for this couple is just 62 per cent of their pre-retirement earnings, they can increase their regular consumption by $14,000 a year, which represents an increase of 43 per cent!

DETAILS ON THE CALCULATIONS

Some expenses have been adjusted for purposes of these calculations. Child-raising expenses, for instance, are usually concentrated in a 21-year window. We spread them over a 35-year period, effectively pro-rating them. Similarly, mortgage payments are often made over a 25-year period and, once again, the amount shown is pro-rated by dividing it over 35 years.

The couple in the example rolled over their RRSP account balance into a Registered Retirement Income Fund (RRIF), from which they draw an annual income. We assumed that the RRIF will earn an annual return of 5.75 per cent after expenses, and that the couple will withdraw amounts as necessary in order to maintain an income stream that grows with inflation. The alternative involves purchasing an annuity, an option that few retirees take (we'll explain why in a later chapter). We also assumed that retirement income will rise annually at the same rate as inflation, which we pegged at 2.25 per cent annually.

The income the couple draws from their retirement savings will be higher in the first five years of retirement because we

---

assume they will postpone collecting their CPP until age 70, when the CPP benefit has considerably greater value than if payments start at 60 or 65. Delaying the payments represents no hardship to the couple because they can draw more from their RRIF until 70 to make up for the absence of CPP income.

Other assumptions include:

- Saving for retirement starts at age 30, and the savings rate is a fixed 6.5 per cent of pay.

- The couple did not participate in a workplace pension plan.

- The CPP benefit to which each spouse is entitled is 90 per cent of the maximum expected at their earnings level meaning they had more years of low or no earnings than could be accommodated under the CPP dropout rules.

What About Trying to Reach 70 Per Cent?

Even though the first example showed that a retirement target of 62 per cent provides ample retirement income, let's see what happens if the same couple had actually saved enough to reach the 70 per cent target that some advisors feel is necessary. To achieve that goal, the couple would have to change three aspects of their spending habits over the 35-year period between age 30 and age 65. They would have to do the following:

- Contribute more to their RRSP—about 8.5 per cent of their pay for 35 years instead of 6.5 per cent

- Reduce other expenditures to make up for the larger RRSP contributions, for example, by buying a less expensive house and cutting their mortgage payment from 25 per cent to 22 per cent of income

- Cut other expenses, including those associated with raising their children

Perhaps their son would have to forgo playing organized hockey and their daughter would not be able to take piano lessons (or vice versa), and both would have to do with fewer new clothes. With these types of cost-cutting measures, the cost of raising the children could fall from 20 to 18 per cent of income.

Table 10.2 shows the results with our new assumptions. Reaching their target of 70 per cent of pre-retirement income produces $54,300 annually before tax from RRSPs, CPP, and OAS.

Table 10.2: Couple with House and Two Children, Average Third-Quintile Income

Retirement at Age 65— All Amounts Rounded	Before Retirement	After Retirement
Total annual income before taxes	$78,000	$54,300
Less RRSP contributions (8.5% of pay)	($6,600)	0
Less CPP contributions	($3,500)	0
Less child-raising costs	($8,400)	0
Less mortgage payments	($12,300)	0
Less employment expenses including EI premiums	($3,700)	0
Less income tax and provincial health premium	($9,300)	($2,700)
Income available for regular consumption	**$34,200**	**$51,600**

Their after-tax retirement income of $51,600 enables the retired couple to spend 50 per cent more ($51,600 versus $34,200) on regular consumption in their retirement years than they spent when they were working. To reach this goal, they had to pinch pennies for 35 years, which affected their own lifestyle and that of their children. Now that they have endured half a lifetime of being careful with money, now that their children have grown up and left home, and now that they are on the verge of old age, do we really think they will start spending 50 per cent more than they used to spend? Did it really make sense to be so frugal for so long to reach this position? For middle-income savers who are relying on RRSPs for their retirement, a 70 per cent retirement target is rational only if they agree they want a much more lavish lifestyle after they retire than they ever enjoyed while they worked.

If Not 70 Per Cent, Then What?

It's time to determine a new retirement income target, one more geared to your actual needs than the widely promoted 70 per cent rule. No actuary likes to be tied down to one number but it is fair to say that a 50 per cent retirement income target is a lot closer to what's really needed than 70 per cent. We will show why in the next chapter.

11

The Neutral Retirement Income Target

The previous chapter showed the connection between retirement income and the income you have available for regular consumption before retirement. The more you save for retirement, the less you have left for regular consumption during your working years. Conservatism generally is a good thing where financial matters are concerned but it can be carried too far. When the couple in the last chapter set their retirement target at 70 per cent, they ended up with a very meagre existence in the 35 years preceding their retirement. People generally do not want to deprive themselves throughout their working career just to have a higher level of income in retirement than they'll actually spend.

If 70 per cent isn't the right number, and we want to arrive at a more reasonable retirement target, we can't just pick a number out of the air. The *right* number has to come with a story. The best story, perhaps, is that we should strive to have enough retirement income to be able to continue the same level of regular consumption that we enjoyed before retirement. This at least is a good starting point;

some people will want higher income in retirement while others will expect it to be somewhat lower. We'll call the income target that balances both positions the Neutral Retirement Income Target or NRIT. The NRIT is the retirement income, expressed as a percentage of final pre-retirement gross income, that provides for the same consumption before and after retirement.

The NRIT differs somewhat from person to person because it depends on various factors including income level, home ownership, and number of children. In the following examples, we will continue to assume that people are planning to reach their NRIT by saving through their RRSP. Looking at the same middle-income couple we saw in Chapter 10, we find that a savings rate of just 2.1 per cent yields roughly the same ongoing consumption before and after retirement.

Table 11.1: Couple with House and Two Children, Average Third-Quintile Income

Retirement at Age 65—All Amounts Rounded	Before Retirement	After Retirement
Total annual income before taxes	$78,000	$35,600
Less RRSP contributions (2.1% of pay)	($1,600)	0
Less CPP contributions	($3,500)	0
Less child-raising costs	($9,400)	0
Less mortgage payments	($13,900)	0
Less employment expenses including EI premiums	($3,700)	0
Less income tax and provincial health premium	($10,300)	0
Income available for regular consumption	**$35,600**	**$35,600**

The NRIT here is 46 per cent, being the ratio of $35,600 (retirement income) to $78,000 (pre-retirement pay). The retirement target of 46 per cent is considered to be neutral for this couple because it affords them the same level of consumption before and after retirement. Again, it appears remarkable that $35,600 in retirement income produces the same regular ongoing consumption as $78,000 of pre-retirement earnings, but we already explained in the last chapter why a low level of retirement income can go such a long way. It all comes down to the specific pre-retirement expenditures described in Chapter 10. Figure 11.1 illustrates in more graphic form why the NRIT is so low.

Figure 11.1: Why Retirement Income Target Is So Low

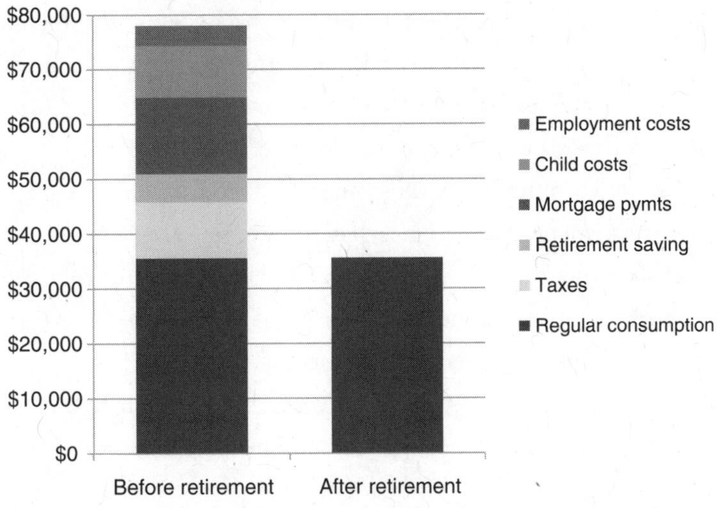

It is equally remarkable that they need to save just 2.1 per cent of pay in their RRSP to achieve their NRIT. Notice that this couple is paying no income taxes after retirement, one of the less-appreciated tax advantages of being 65 or older in Canada. In this case, they are making use of their pension income credit (up to $2,000 each), the age 65 credit (up to $6,720 each), and the ability to split income and share credits between spouses, something they could not do before they retired. It should be noted that retirees are eligible for the pension income credit, income-splitting, and credit-sharing at any retirement age before or after 65; only the age credit depends on attaining age 65.

Challenging the NRIT Concept

The idea that the retirement income target can be below 50 per cent of employment income without measurably affecting lifestyle is so foreign that it is natural to look for holes in the argument. Some people will point out that expenses, such as paying off the mortgage or raising children, do not end precisely at the point of retirement, which is true. You may have paid off your house while still in your fifties, and your children may become self-supporting years before you retire (although anecdotal evidence says don't count on it!). If that's the case, the income available for consumption during the window between the end of those major expenditures and the beginning of retirement can be higher than our example suggests. But this is balanced by other years when child-raising costs and mortgage payments were even higher than our model shows. In those years, income available for consumption was even less, which means the couple may not have been able to save anything in their RRSP, and in fact may have gone deeper in debt. If some of those expenditures have eased off in the years immediately prior to retirement, it is an opportunity to pay off debt and play catch-up with extra contributions to the RRSP to make up for the lost years. There may be no consumption bonanza in that window period after all.

Another potential criticism is that the economic assumptions used to determine the NRIT are too optimistic. We think they are fairly realistic and, in fact, some people would say they are on the pessimistic side. For instance, the mortgage payments and child-raising costs could both have been higher which would have led to even lower NRITs.

Looking at Other Situations

The previous example showed that a middle-income couple with a house and two children would not have real difficulty saving enough in an RRSP to enjoy the same lifestyle after retirement, assuming they start saving at a consistent rate of pay by the time they're 30, or make up for years of missed RRSP contributions when disposable income is larger. Now let's examine what happens with other situations, such as:

- a higher-income household;
- a retirement age earlier than 65;
- a two-earner couple with no children;
- a single person saving for retirement.

Higher-Income Families

Instead of a couple with third-quintile income, let's consider a couple with total annual income of $110,000 which places them within the fourth quintile, meaning only 20 per cent of Canadian households earn more per year. Their higher income means they will have a heavier tax burden in their pre-retirement years. Since government pensions will constitute a smaller percentage of their overall retirement income, the asset balance in RRSPs will be more important in ensuring their retirement security. RRSP savings rates thus will have to be higher than in the previous example, but of course this couple should have a commensurately greater ability to save.

As it turns out, this level of household earnings is very close to the sweet spot for taking full advantage of the tax system. At retirement, the couple can make full use of their pension income credit and nearly full use of the age credit. At the same time, their retirement income is not high enough to be affected by the OAS clawback. Performing the calculations, we find they can achieve their NRIT with RRSP contributions of 3.8 per cent of household income over a 35-year period, as shown in Table 11.2. Obviously, this is more than the 2.1 per cent savings rate in the first example, but not much more.

Table 11.2: Couple with House and Two Children, Average Fourth-Quintile Income

Retirement at Age 65—All Amounts Rounded	Before Retirement	After Retirement
Total annual income before taxes	$110,000	$48,300
Less RRSP contributions (3.8% of pay)	($4,200)	0
Less CPP contributions	($4,200)	0
Less child-raising costs	($13,200)	0
Less mortgage payments	($19,600)	0
Less employment expenses including EI premiums	($4,900)	0
Less income tax and provincial health premium	($17,300)	($1,600)
Income available for regular consumption	**$46,600**	**$46,700**

With total retirement income of $48,300 against pre-retirement earnings of $110,000, their NRIT is 44 per cent, lower than for the third-quintile couple because the reduction in income taxes after retirement has a bigger impact for higher earners.

Now let's look at a fifth-quintile household in Table 11.3, representing the top 20 per cent of Canadian households whose average total annual income is $204,000.

Table 11.3: Couple with House and Two Children, Average Fifth-Quintile Income

Retirement at Age 65—All Amounts Rounded	Before Retirement	After Retirement
Total annual income before taxes	$204,000	$83,500
Less RRSP contributions (6.5% of pay)	($13,300)	0
Less CPP contributions	($4,600)	0
Less child-raising costs	($24,500)	0
Less mortgage payments	($36,400)	0
Less employment expenses including EI premiums	($7,800)	0
Less income tax and provincial health premium	($43,700)	($8,900)
Income available for regular consumption	**$73,700**	**$74,600**

With retirement income of $83,500 before income tax against pre-retirement income of $204,000, this couple's NRIT is just 41 per cent. In general, the higher the income level, the lower the Neutral Retirement Income Target.

Retiring Early

In the previous examples, we assumed retirement occurred at 65. While earlier chapters suggest this will eventually become our reality, the average retirement age in Canada at this point is still just 62. In Table 11.4, we will recalculate the NRIT for the third-quintile couple from Table 11.1, this time assuming that retirement occurs at 62 instead of 65. We will continue to assume that the primary residence is paid for and the children are no longer dependent on their parents.

The working career is now three years shorter, which concentrates all those pre-retirement expenses, such as mortgage payments and child-related expenditures, over a shorter period. We will spread those expenditures over just 32 years instead of 35. Since earlier retirement means fewer years to accumulate retirement savings, the required savings rate has to be higher. The final RRSP balance also has to be higher, because the couple will receive payments for three years longer than if they retired at 65. Finally, they will also face greater tax liability because the age 65 credit will not apply immediately..

Table 11.4: Couple with House and Two Children, Average Third-Quintile Income

Retirement at Age 65—All Amounts Rounded	Before Retirement	After Retirement
Total annual income before taxes	$78,000	$32,800
Less RRSP contributions (3.5% of pay)	($2,700)	0
Less CPP contributions	($3,500)	0
Less child-raising costs	($10,200)	0
Less mortgage payments	($15,200)	0
Less employment expenses including EI premiums	($3,700)	0
Less income tax and provincial health premium	($10,100)	0
Income available for regular consumption	**$32,600**	**$32,800**

Their NRIT is 42 per cent, which is about 4 per cent lower than if they retired at 65. While the couple needed to put only 2.1 per cent into an RRSP each year to reach their NRIT at 65, they will now need to save 3.5 per cent of their income each year. The bad news is that their retirement income has dropped from the $35,600 they could expect when retiring at 65 to only $32,800. They also had less disposable income during their working years because they needed to contribute more to their RRSP, and had a shorter period to pay off their mortgage and amortize child-related costs. Retiring early doesn't just mean less income in retirement, it also means less disposable income throughout your working career while you make the sacrifices necessary to save enough. By planning to retire early, the couple reconciled themselves to a lower standard of living. Since they have essentially lowered the bar, the NRIT is lower.

Earlier retirement is possible if you are ready to accept a lower standard of living both throughout your working years and into retirement. Table 11.5 suggests your disposable income drops by about 3 per cent for each year that you decide to retire earlier. If you are planning to retire at 65 or later, it is a good idea to save a little more than is needed to reach your NRIT. That is because you never know when your plans might change and you are forced to retire earlier than you expected. And if you stick to your plan to retire at 65, you'll have a little extra income!

Table 11.5: How Disposable Income Drops with Earlier Retirement

Total household income	Income Available for Regular Consumption		
	Retire at 65	Retire at 62	% drop
Third-quintile earnings ($78,000)	$35,600	$32,600	8%
Fourth-quintile earnings ($110,000)	$46,600	$42,600	8%
Fifth-quintile earnings ($204,000)	$73,700	$66,700	9%

The converse also holds true. The longer you are prepared to postpone your retirement, the higher your standard of living, assuming you keep on saving until you retire. The ideal balance between picking the right retirement age and the right standard of living will be different for everyone.

No Children

A couple without children will have higher income available for regular consumption, so they can spend more money on themselves. Not surprisingly, they will need to save more if they wish to continue that higher standard of living into retirement, yielding a higher NRIT than a couple with children.

If a couple decides to have children, it seems objectionable that they should have to resign themselves to a lower level of consumption for life. The reality, however, is that couples with children do forgo some personal consumption while the children are growing up. Few of us consciously think of making up for this by consuming more after retirement, because the mindset is to preserve an established standard of living, not to improve on it. Besides, trying to make up for forgone consumption in one's retirement years by saving more during the working years simply drops the pre-retirement standard of living even further.

Still, the issue of forgone consumption might lead some couples to choose a target that is a little different than their NRIT. They might want a better lifestyle in retirement than they enjoyed while working and raising their children, which means their retirement income target should be a little higher than their NRIT. The only question is, how much more pre-retirement consumption are they prepared to give up?

Going the other way is much easier. Childless couples might be prepared to settle for somewhat lower consumption in retirement, perhaps somewhere between their own NRIT and the NRIT for a couple with children. This might appeal to them because it allows them to spend a little more during their working lives or, alternatively, it gives them the option to retire earlier.

Table 11.6: Couple with House and No Children, Average Third-Quintile Income

Retirement at Age 65—All Amounts Rounded	Before Retirement	After Retirement
Total annual income before taxes	$78,000	$43,500
Less RRSP contributions (4.7% of pay)	($3,700)	0
Less CPP contributions	($3,500)	0
Less child-raising costs	0	0
Less mortgage payments	($13,900)	0
Less employment expenses including EI premiums	($3,700)	0
Less income tax and provincial health premium	($10,400)	($700)
Income available for regular consumption	**$42,800**	**$42,800**

In Table 11.6, notice that the NRIT is much higher if one doesn't have children, rising here to 56 per cent from the 46 per cent we saw for a couple with two children. To reach their NRIT, the necessary savings rate for the childless couple is 4.7 per cent annually for 35 years. The good news is that they have more disposable income to make it happen, and their standard of living during their working years as well as their retirement years will be considerably better than if they had children. (Fortunately for the human race, there is more to life than money.)

We get essentially the same result at higher income levels. The NRIT for the fourth-quintile couple we saw earlier rises from 44 per cent (see Table 11.2) to 55 per cent if we assume no children, and their required savings rate jumps from 3.8 per cent to 6.9 per cent.

A Single Person

An individual without a spouse or dependent children and the same $78,000 in household earnings will have a higher NRIT than a couple with children because they have lower pre-retirement expenses to cut into their regular consumption. Besides no child-related expenses, they might also have lower mortgage payments than the married-with-children household because they don't need as large a home. Assuming their mortgage payments are 20 per cent less, the single individual's NRIT would be 55 per cent, very close to the couple with no children in the previous example. Marital status doesn't make much of a difference; having children, however, makes a big difference.

Lower-Income Households

To this point we have looked at households where the total income falls in the third, fourth, or fifth quintile, which represent the top 60 per cent of Canadian households by income level. The retirement planning process is quite different for those in the bottom 40 per cent, who have a much harder time finding money to save for retirement. Fortunately, the need to save is smaller as well, since Old Age Security and the Guaranteed Income Supplement often provide as much income as the householders enjoyed when they were working. To the extent they can save for retirement, they should use a Tax-Free Savings Account rather than an RRSP, as we'll see in a later chapter.

12

Arriving at Your Own Retirement Income Target

We have learned that a reasonable retirement income target for most people is significantly less than 70 per cent of one's final year's income. Chapter 11 showed what the neutral retirement income target (NRIT) would be in a variety of situations. In this chapter, we help you define your own retirement income target and then provide some guidance as to how to reach it.

Rule of Thumb

The examples in the last chapter showed that the NRIT ranged from as low as 41 per cent for the high-income couple with children to as high as 56 per cent for the middle-income couple with no children. In fact it can be a little lower than 41 per cent at very high income levels, and it can be a little higher than 56 per cent for middle-income people with no children who choose to rent rather than buy their home. For the vast majority, the range is between 40 per cent and 60 per cent.

At the risk of oversimplifying, you might take 50 per cent as the starting point for estimating your own retirement income target. This assumes you are in the middle- to high-income range because a higher target is necessary for lower-income Canadians. You can then refine that target by subtracting up to 10 percentage points if all of the following conditions are satisfied: (a) your household income is well above average; (b) you own a home and will pay off the mortgage by the time you retire; and (c) you have children who will have left home by the time you retire. Alternatively, you would add up to 10 percentage points if none of those conditions apply. If some of the conditions apply and some don't, you can assume your NRIT will hover somewhere around the 50 per cent level. This rule is not perfect but it is significantly better than the old 70 per cent rule.

Modifying the Rule

Having established the general rule for approximating your NRIT, we can now describe some situations that can move your own target higher or lower.

Pillar 4 Assets

Our calculations in Chapter 11 assume that the couples are trying to reach their retirement income goals solely with government pensions (Pillars 1 and 2) plus any income they can generate from RRSPs (part of Pillar 3). As we saw in Chapter 2, many people hold considerable wealth in the form of other assets that are outside of the three pillars. To the extent you possess so-called Pillar 4 assets that you are prepared to convert into income at retirement, you can save less than we have shown and still achieve your NRIT.

Pension Plan Coverage

If you're covered under a pension plan at your workplace, consider yourself lucky. Depending upon the plan, it will reduce or even eliminate your need to save for retirement through RRSPs because your employer is making contributions on your behalf. This frees up disposable income available for regular consumption before retirement. In a nutshell, participation in a workplace pension plan gives you a higher NRIT, which you will most likely want to maintain in retirement.

Buying an Annuity

The examples in the previous chapter assumed the couples would be transferring their RRSP monies to a RRIF at retirement and then drawing an income from the RRIF for life. In your case, if you choose to purchase an annuity instead, you will need to save more to reach your goal. That is because annuities are virtually risk-free and eliminating risk comes at a cost, which in this case takes the form of contributing more to an RRSP over your working life. This doesn't make it wrong to buy an annuity. By eliminating risk, you might sleep better. Just because a RRIF portfolio invested in stocks and bonds is *expected* to provide a better return during your retirement doesn't necessarily mean it will. The next few chapters will have more to say about investment risk and choosing your investments.

Reduced Income Needs In Phase 2

In Chapter 8, we learned that your income needs might drop substantially in the second phase of your retirement, a time when you will be less able to get around and will have fewer opportunities to spend your money. In our NRIT calculations, we have conservatively assumed that your RRSP assets will be converted into retirement income that rises with inflation throughout your retirement, but the conclusions about one's spending habits in the second phase suggest this is overkill. By saving more than you need, your disposable income during your working years will end up being lower than necessary. Alternatively, you will be spending less in Phase 1 of retirement than you can afford to spend. Rather than change the calculations and lower the savings rate, we have left the numbers the same, but bear in mind that this is one more reason why our calculations are on the conservative side.

Provision for Adverse Deviation

What if your investment return is different than you predicted when estimating your NRIT and calculating the corresponding RRSP savings rate? It is a certainty it will be different, you just won't know how different until you are on the verge of retirement. Even then, you won't know because your investment return after retirement is also an unknown. Actuaries make some allowance for this by building in a margin of safety, which they call a "provision for adverse deviation." For instance, if your best estimate calculation indicates you should be saving 6 per cent a year, you might bump it up to 7 per cent. You should not go too far in terms of over-saving, however, since it could seriously lower your living standard before retirement.

Summary

Below is a summary of the various reasons to pick a retirement income target that is higher than your NRIT:

- You have reason to believe you may live longer than normal (good health, regular fitness regimen, longevity runs in the family, etc.) so your savings will have to last longer.
- Your target is based on retiring at 65 but you might change your mind and retire earlier, or your employer might push you out before you reach 65.

- You want a little cushion in case your RRSP balance comes in below your projections.

- Your RRSP will be invested more conservatively than normal, or you plan to buy an annuity. In either case you might not achieve the investment returns we have used in our calculations.

- There is a chance your marital status might change and a separation would worsen your financial situation.

- You expect you will have to help take care of aged parents.

Here are reasons to pick a target that is lower than your NRIT:

- You have reason to believe your life expectancy is shorter than usual.

- You accept the notion that your spending will decline when you enter into the second phase of retirement (see Chapter 8).

- You prefer to frontload your consumption, meaning you would rather spend more while you are still young and in return, live a more modest lifestyle later on.

- By retirement, you will have significant Pillar 4 assets to supplement your income.

- You expect to inherit a significant amount at some point.

Choosing a Savings Rate

So far we have concentrated on retirement income targets. These are not much use in retirement planning unless you also know the savings rate you need to reach those targets. We showed the savings rates in several examples in Chapter 11. Figure 12.1 shows how the savings rates needed to reach the NRIT vary by income level. These have been calculated in the case of a two-earner couple with two children and a home.

Figure 12.1: Savings Rate—Couple with Two Children

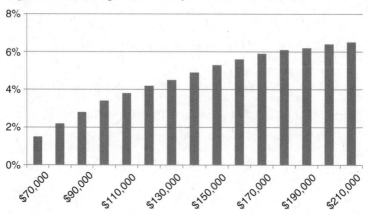

The savings rate ranges between 2 and 7 per cent of pay, rising by about 1 per cent of pay for every $30,000 of household income. Remember that this contribution would have to be made every year for 35 years in order to pay for retirement at 65. Miss a year and double the amount would have to be contributed in the following year. So while the contribution rates may not seem too high, the relentless saving schedule makes it a little more challenging.

Figure 12.2 shows the RRSP balance that one should have by age 65 to generate the income needed to reach the NRIT. These balances correspond to the savings rates in Figure 12.1.

The RRSP account balance needed ranges from under $100,000 to a little over $700,000. This is why there is no simple answer to the question, how much does one need in RRSP savings to have a comfortable retirement? There is, however, a reasonably simple formula to approximate what you need. For a couple in this situation with household earnings of at least $70,000, their RRSP balance needs to be about $40,000 plus five times the portion of their household income in excess of $75,000.

Appendix C shows the savings rates and account balances for the situation of a two-earner couple with no children. The required

Figure 12.2: RRSP Target at 65—Couple with Two Children

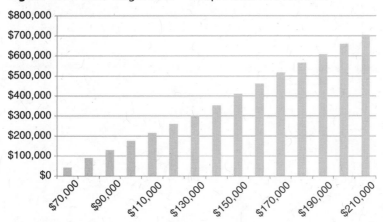

savings rate is about 2 per cent of pay higher across the income spectrum, while the RRSP balance needed at 65 is higher as well. This is a counter-intuitive result: if you do not have children, your savings target will be higher. The reason is that a childless couple can spend more on themselves in the pre-retirement phase. If they wish to keep up this higher level of spending after retirement, they will need more money.

Reaching Your NRIT

With your NRIT goal established, how do you make sure you reach it? One scenario would require you to adjust your savings rate down or up every so often, depending on whether your investments perform better or worse than you expected. As we saw in Chapter 6, though, this is probably *not* what you would do because people do not tend to change their savings rate just because investment results have been poor. Most people are more likely to change their retirement age before they change their savings rate. Of course, investing your retirement savings wisely will make the task easier. The investment process is discussed in the next four chapters.

13

Investment Basics

To this point, we have been using the term "saving" when it comes to building the assets you need to fund your retirement. If only it were that simple! It would be easy if all you had to do was earmark a part of each paycheque for deposit into your RRSP and then forget about it until it comes time to reap the rewards at retirement. Unfortunately, you need to make some decisions along the way about how the monies you've saved can best be invested. We say it's unfortunate because investing is causing more anxiety and head-scratching these days than has been the case for a long time. For instance, the investment-counselling firm, BlackRock, reveals that more than two-thirds of investors with more than $100,000 in investable assets feel "much less confident" about the investment decisions they make now than they did in the past.

The anxiety comes from the roller-coaster ride experienced by investors when the stock markets fell 50 per cent in a 10-month span ending in March 2009 and then rose 100 per cent in the subsequent 24 months, only to be afflicted by a Euro-malaise which may linger for some time yet. As for the head-scratching, how can one achieve a decent investment return when bonds are yielding less than 3 per cent, and bank deposits less than 1 per cent? There was a time when a long-term return of 9 per cent didn't seem outlandish. By contrast, the pension projections in this book are based on RRSPs earning an annual return of 5.75 per cent net of fees. Even this level of return is going to be a challenge to obtain and entails some risk.

You might think you could wash your hands of all decision-making by hiring a financial advisor to manage your portfolio, but the fact is that you need to stay involved. Even if you hire an advisor, you should still have a basic knowledge of investments so that you can communicate your goals properly. Being better informed will also enable you to assess the performance of your portfolio and, perhaps best of all, sleep a little better at night.

Investment Horizon

The starting point is to know the period over which you need to achieve your investment results—your "investment horizon." When saving for retirement, the investment horizon is usually measured in decades. If the stock market makes us anxious, it is because we tend to fret too much over short-term price gyrations, even though they are hardly more than noise in the longer run.

The strange thing is that most of us have an intuitive understanding of our investment horizon when it comes to the investment in our home. If a homeowner hears that house prices might be due for a fall, the typical answer is, "I'm not moving anytime soon so a drop in prices doesn't matter to me." The same person, however, may very well have an anxiety attack over a 300-point drop in the stock market, even if he has no plans to retire for 20 years. In fact, the two situations are the same and the homeowner's attitude is the one we need to adopt when investing our retirement savings.

Your investment horizon dictates your choice of investments. If you had $100 in your pocket today and absolutely needed to make sure you had $100 on hand in a week's time to pay off a loan, you would be smart to leave the money in cash. An investment horizon of one week dictates investing in cash. On the other hand, if you needed that $100 to grow to $200 over the next 10 years, you would invest in something that had a chance of growing to $200 in that time frame, and it wouldn't be cash.

If you are planning to use your retirement savings to purchase an annuity at retirement, your investment horizon will be the number of years until the annuity purchase date, or perhaps a little shorter than that, because you should be gradually reducing your risk in the years leading up to the annuity purchase to ensure that a last-second stock market correction doesn't derail your plans.

If you don't plan to use your RRSP balance to buy an annuity at retirement, you will continue to control your investments, possibly for the rest of your life. In this case, your investment horizon will be considerably longer than the time remaining until retirement. For instance, if you are 50, your horizon would be closer to 30 years. All other things being equal, this means you should be prepared to invest in funds that have a higher expected return, even if it means bigger price swings in the shorter term.

Getting Comfortable with Risk

People tend to avoid risk if they can. That is why we buy insurance and wear seatbelts. Sometimes, the potential payoff is big enough that we can overcome our aversion to risk. In a lottery, for example, the risk (the price of a lottery ticket) is small and the payoff is large, albeit unlikely. An example that is more relevant for our purposes is investing our savings in securities or funds that could suffer a loss, such as an equity fund.[1] We expose ourselves to risk in this case because it gives us the chance of a payoff that is better than if we didn't take any risk.

Another type of risk to watch for is credit risk. This can be more deadly than stock market losses simply because the loss is sudden and usually permanent. An example of credit risk is holding a second mortgage for an acquaintance. A mortgage seems to provide the lender with a steady income, but what if the mortgagee suddenly loses his job or gets sick and can`t make the payments? You stand to lose your investment and all for the sake of a little more return than you would earn from a safer investment. If you still want to take a chance, credit risk can at least be minimized by investing in a fund that holds enough medium-to-low quality securities (such as high-yield bonds) so that if one investment goes bad, it won't have a devastating impact on your overall return.

No matter how much investment knowledge you have, you won't really be able to avoid risk entirely. Risk and return are closely related. You usually need to take more risk if you want a higher return. It is no guarantee of a higher return—if it were, there wouldn't be any risk—but without taking on risk, your long-term return will almost certainly be much less than you will need to meet your goals. Imagine a 35-year-old who decided in 1981 that stocks were too risky and invested in a high-yield savings account instead. Over the 30-year period ending December 2011, his account balance would have gone up 110 per cent. Had he invested in equities, he would have earned more than 1,200 per cent in the same period. The result would be similar over almost any 30-year period in the past 70 years.

This is where your risk tolerance needs to be considered. Actuaries aside, people are not automatons. It is difficult to stay calm in the midst of a financial storm such as the 2008 financial crisis. If you understand the concepts of investment horizon and risk and you still lose sleep over your investments, it is an indication you should be choosing a less aggressive asset mix, meaning one that is less heavily weighted in equities. To measure your own risk tolerance, you should make use of a self-assessment questionnaire which you can obtain through your financial advisor, investment manager, or if you participate in a group plan, your plan administrator. Below is a sample of the investment risk questionnaire that Morneau Shepell offers to participants in RRSPs and other capital accumulation plans.

INVESTOR PROFILE QUESTIONNAIRE

This questionnaire is designed to measure how aggressively you should invest your retirement savings, given your financial situation and your personal sensitivity to short-term fluctuations in investment returns. It uses the information you provide to suggest an investment mix that suits your investor profile.

Question 1

When do you expect to retire?

A. In less than 5 years

B. Between 5 and 14 years from now

C. Between 15 and 24 years from now

D. In 25 years or more

Question 2

Which of the following statements best describes your disposable income at the moment?

A. I need all of my disposable income to cover living expenses and I find it hard to meet my debt payments

B. My disposable income covers living expenses and debts, but leaves very little for savings

C. I can put money aside for upcoming expenses and for retirement

D. My disposable income allows for substantial savings

Question 3

How would you describe your current financial situation?

A. I have substantial debt and little or no savings

B. I am reducing my debt and I have some small savings

C. I have nearly repaid my debt and my savings are growing more rapidly

D. I have little or no debt and I have substantial savings

E. I have little or no debt, but I have little or no savings either

Important: If you own a residence, your debt excludes your mortgage and the value of your residence is not considered as savings.

Question 4

How do your total retirement savings compare with your annual retirement savings contributions? My total retirement savings represent . . .

A. Less than 5 times my annual contributions

B. Between 6 and 10 times my annual contributions

C. Between 11 and 20 times my annual contributions

D. More than 20 times my annual contributions

Question 5

Which of the following statements best describes how you currently invest your personal retirement savings?

A. I have no retirement savings
B. I am not sure how my retirement savings are invested
C. I invest in conservative vehicles such as guaranteed investment certificates (GICs) or government bonds
D. I invest mainly in a range of mutual funds, with or without the help of an investment advisor or financial planner
E. I manage my personal investments—which include stocks and equity funds—myself

Question 6

Think of the total value of your retirement savings. How much of a drop in that value could you tolerate over a one-year period without becoming anxious?

A. I could not tolerate any drop
B. I could tolerate a drop of up to 5%
C. I could tolerate a drop of up to 10%
D. I could tolerate a drop of up to 15%
E. I could tolerate a drop of more than 15% over a one-year period—I am invested for the long-term

Question 7

It is common knowledge that the value of investment funds varies over time. Imagine that you invested a large sum in a mutual fund last year. Since then, the fund has lost 20% of its value, despite very solid long-term historical performance. This decrease in value is consistent with the performance of similar investment funds over the same period. What would you do in this situation?

A. I would take my money out of the fund before I lost any more
B. I would take half my money out of the fund
C. I would do nothing in the hopes that the fund would go back up and I would suffer no actual loss
D. I would take advantage of the drop to put more money into the fund

Imagine that a quarter of your total retirement savings, or $10,000, were invested in this fund. This investment would now be worth $8,000. How would you deal with this situation?

Question 8

If you had to put all your savings in one of the four portfolios (or investment baskets) shown below, which would you choose? A portfolio that, over the next three years, would generate an average annual return:

A. Portfolio 1: between 2% and 4%
B. Portfolio 2: between 0% and 8%
C. Portfolio 3: between −3% and 12%
D. Portfolio 4: between −5% and 20%

Question 9

When you retire, what will drive how you convert your retirement savings into income?

A. Security
B. Flexibility
C. Security and flexibility
D. Flexibility in the early years, security in the later years
E. I have no idea at the moment

Your Score

Tabulate your score in the following tables.

Question	A	B	C	D	E	Your score
1	0	3	5	7	-	
2	0	1	2	3	-	
3	0	2	4	6	5	
4	3	2	0	3	-	
5	2	2	0	3	5	
6	0	3	4	5	6	
7	0	2	4	5	-	
8	0	1	2	3	-	
Questions 1–8 total:						(A)

For question 9, pick one of the following based on how you answered question 1.

Your answer	A	B	C	D	E	Your score
< 5 years	0	10	5	7	5	
5–14 years	5	10	7	8	7	
15–25 years	10	12	10	10	10	
> 25 years	10	12	10	10	10	
Question 9 total:						(B)

Now tabulate your score: (A) + (B) = Total.

Your Results

If your score was …	You are this type of investor …
Between 0 and 10	Cautious
Between 11 and 20	Conservative
Between 21 and 30	Moderate
Between 31 and 40	Dynamic
Between 41 and 50	Aggressive

The following shows you how a typical, well-informed investor would allocate his/her savings between the various asset categories. Find your resulting profile below to see how you could invest your savings.

Score	Profile	How savings could be allocated		
		Bonds	Cdn Equity	Foreign Equity
0 to 10	Cautious	80%	10%	10%
11 to 20	Conservative	65%	17.5%	17.5%
21 to 30	Moderate	50%	25%	25%
31 to 40	Dynamic	34%	33%	33%
41 to 50	Aggressive	20%	40%	40%

> **Remarks**
> Your investment needs may change from time to time. You should redo this exercise at regular intervals or when your personal and financial situation changes.

Focus on Real Returns

During the 1970s, the median investment return realized by pension fund managers was 6.1 per cent annually. Sound good? It was terrible, because the annual inflation rate during the same period averaged 7.5 per cent. If your return is less than inflation, you are losing ground. Always focus on "real returns," that is, the return on investment after inflation has been accounted for, rather than "nominal returns," which don't take inflation into account. This is especially important, of course, in times of high inflation.

Investment Options: Good, Bad, and Indifferent

When you invest your RRSP savings, you are at the mercy of the capital markets. Stock markets do crash from time to time, and can temporarily wipe out many years of gains over a short period. The financial crisis of 2008 scared many investors away from the stock market. Even four years later, a *Toronto Star* survey showed that six in 10 Ontarians believe they don't have to invest in the stock market to grow their retirement nest egg. Some of them no doubt lost money in the stock market in recent years and then fled to the apparent safety of second mortgages and real estate investments, perhaps by purchasing and renting out condominiums. They may be about to find out what risk is!

The most common alternative to stocks is bonds, which are also subject to losses from time to time, just not quite as often or as large as for stocks. With the steady drops in interest rates over the past

30 years, bond prices have risen (bond prices always move in the opposite direction to interest rates). Still, even bonds involve risk. A rise in interest rates would send bond prices plummeting.

So it's understandable if you want to get off the investment roller coaster. Unfortunately, this is easier said than done. You can't keep all your money in cash, treasury bills, guaranteed interest certificates (GICs), Canada Savings Bonds, or bank savings accounts for the long term, because the real return will be close to zero. It could even be negative. You will find that investing in equities and longer-term bonds is a practical necessity, so we should get better acquainted with their basic characteristics.

Equities Are Better than They Look

Stock markets have been extremely volatile over the short term, but they remain consistently the best bet over longer periods. Many people believe, however, that the last decade has been an extraordinarily bad time to invest in equities and that it promises to be equally bad in future years. With iconic companies like Lehman Brothers failing, potential defaults by European countries, and trillion-dollar bailouts to keep economies functioning, are we living in times of unprecedented uncertainty and risk? Is it possible that the future for equities will be fundamentally different from the last 200 years?

Those are reasonable questions, and all we can do is make the observation that the best times for investing have historically occurred when fear is rampant. Fear of an economic collapse was perhaps most intense in March 2009, which is just when markets began turning around. Since then, the stock market has climbed about 100 per cent, leaving the investors who bailed out of the falling market feeling both chagrined and a little less wealthy.

How often does the stock market actually produce a loss in a given year? The first decade of the twenty-first century seemed like a period of unprecedented volatility, yet it does not seem particularly exceptional if one simply counts the number of years when Canadian equities would have lost money (in nominal terms).

Table 13.1: Table, as follows: Stock Market Gyrations

Decade	Number of Calendar Years of Negative Returns
1930s	4
1940s	2
1950s	2
1960s	3
1970s	2
1980s	2
1990s	4
2000s	3

As Table 13.1 shows, it appears we can expect negative returns on equities two to three calendar years out of every 10. Even in the 1990s, which produced heady returns for anyone who stayed fully invested for the entire period, investors would have lost money during four out of the 10 years. This sounds terrible, but as long as one expects it and as long as the longer-term direction for stocks is steadily upward, it is only a minor annoyance. When it comes to investing, the destination is more important than the journey. It's better to focus on the results obtained over the entire investment horizon rather than worry too much about short-term volatility. With that in mind, consider this: the average annual real return for equities over the 25-year period ending in December 2011 was 6 per cent.[2] Remember, this was the return after inflation. This excellent result was realized over a period that includes the stock market crash of October 1987, the bursting of the dot-com bubble in 2000, the so-called perfect storm of 2002–2003, and, of course, the financial crisis of 2008.

The real return over 25-year periods has fluctuated widely over time. As Figure 13.1 reveals, the 25-year average has often been more than 6 per cent per annum but not always.

Figure 13.1: Real Returns for Equities over 25-Year Periods

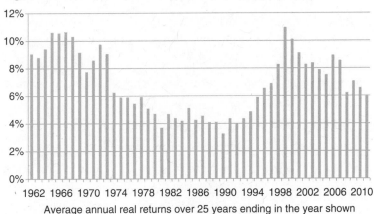

Average annual real returns over 25 years ending in the year shown

The average real return dipped as low as 3.3 per cent annually for the 25-year period ending 1990, and soared as high as 11 per cent for the period ending in 1999. The annual average over all periods, incidentally, was 6.9 per cent, which practically coincides with the average real return going back to 1802.

It is comforting to know that equity returns over 25-year periods since the late 1930s have been reasonably healthy in spite of wars, global oil shocks, various market crashes, at least one stock market bubble, and a scary global financial crisis. That's why it is hard to ignore equities as an investment over the long term.

What About Bonds and Similar Fixed-Income Options?

Fixed-income investments can be either bonds or mortgages. A bond is basically an IOU issued by a government or corporation. Bonds may have a term of up to 30 years and pay a predetermined rate of interest twice each year until the debt is fully repaid at the end of the bond's term, when it is said to have reached "maturity." The "yield" on a bond is the interest rate it is currently paying; the "return" is the sum of the interest received plus the capital gain (or minus the capital loss). Yields are always positive whereas returns can be either positive or negative depending on the capital gain or loss. In pension funds, most bonds are investment grade, which means the issuer is a corporation or government with little chance of defaulting on the debt.

Fixed-income investments typically make up between 30 and 50 per cent of most large pension fund portfolios. They are not expected to provide annual returns as high as equities—that's not their role, although, as we have seen recently, bonds can earn impressive returns under certain circumstances. They help stabilize portfolios, acting like ballast to steady the portfolio and minimize the impact of the year-to-year volatility that occurs with equities. Until recent years, equities tended to produce higher returns than bonds, which is understandable given that equities have traditionally been riskier over shorter periods, so investors expect to earn more money from them to offset the risk.

As Figure 13.2 shows, equities once produced a substantially higher return than bonds, but the difference has been steadily declining since the late 1960s. Bonds performed well because bond yields have been falling for the past 30 years. Falling yields means the prices of previously issued bonds, paying higher interest, have risen, creating capital gains when the bonds are sold, and these capital gains account for the exceptional performance.

Figure 13.2: Excess of 25-Year Average Returns on Equities over Bonds

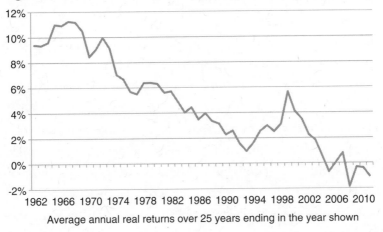

Average annual real returns over 25 years ending in the year shown

If this seems to suggest that bonds are the place to be for your RRSP investment portfolio, that would be a very wrong conclusion. The bull market in bonds is about to come to an abrupt halt, because bond yields are about to reverse direction. Yields may languish for a few years at low levels before they start to climb again, but they have virtually no room to move further downward, thus no capital gain opportunities remain.

Studies indicate that government bond yields go through cycles lasting about 60 years: 30 years for the uptrend and another 30 for the downtrend. While this observation is based on U.S. 10-year government bonds, the same cycle seems to hold true in Canada. As shown in Figure 13.3, yields have been trending exclusively downward for the last 30 years. If the theory holds true, we can expect bond yields to rise for the next 30 years or so, and with each rise in yield of a new bond issue, the price of previously issued bonds will fall, so we can expect bonds to produce much poorer results in the years to come than in the past. Given current yields, it is hard to make the case for investing heavily in long-term government bonds.

High-yield corporate bonds may do somewhat better because the yields are consistently higher. Unlike government bonds, the returns on high-yield bonds come almost exclusively from the interest paid on the bonds rather than on capital gains. For that reason, the returns tend to be higher in times like the present when yields are low and the prospect of capital gains is similarly low. Consider, for example, the RBC Phillips, Hager & North high-yield fund. About 20 per cent of the investments are either A or BBB-rated but the majority are just BB-rated or unrated. Compared with government bonds, there is a higher risk of default on any single holding within the fund, but the fund is diversified enough that the benefit of higher yields tends to outweigh the losses from the odd default. The average annual return over the 10 years to May 31, 2012 was 9.5 per cent before management fees. By comparison, the return of the RBC PH&N bond fund, which is invested mainly in government bonds and higher-quality corporate bonds, was just 6.9 per cent before fees.

Figure 13.3: Yields on 10-Year Canada Bonds

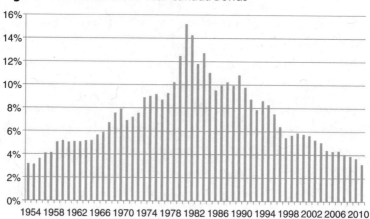

Before we settle on a portfolio that consists solely of equities and bonds, we should at least consider alternative investment classes.

So What Are the Alternatives?

Real estate may seem attractive, at first glance, but it also undergoes major corrections from time to time, including the 1989 collapse of residential real estate prices in Toronto and the bursting of the U.S. housing bubble in 2006, which triggered the 2008 financial crisis that spread worldwide. Since 2006, housing markets have fallen substantially in other parts of the world as well, especially in Europe, so we have to assume that Canada is not immune. We already saw in Chapter 4 that our housing market seems to be especially vulnerable to a correction in the near future. Investing in real estate is problematic for other reasons, including high transaction costs, ongoing taxes, the difficulty of selling quickly in a buyer's market, and the challenges of being a landlord. Still, there is no denying that buying and selling condos would have given a considerably better return than stocks in the past decade.

Instead of actual real estate, second mortgages may appear attractive, due to the higher interest rates they offer. As noted earlier, mortgages introduce credit risk: the higher interest rates paid by the mortgagee come with a higher risk of default, which could ultimately mean the loss of your investment. Mortgages are really like bonds, except the payer is less certain to pay you back.

Another investment category is precious metals, primarily gold and silver, although this category is highly controversial. Precious metals produce no interest and returns are restricted to capital gains, which are by no means assured. No pension fund invests directly in precious metals, and many reputable managers stay away even from investing in gold and silver mining shares.

A few investors with significant capital and experience in the market may do well with alternative investment classes, but in the opinion of the authors, the best alternative for individual investors seeking to build their RRSP remains stocks and bonds or pooled funds that are invested in stocks and bonds.

Determining Your Asset Mix

Your asset mix—the balance of stocks, fixed-income, and cash, as well as any other major investment category—is by far the most important factor in determining the long-term success or failure of your investment strategy. Market timing and buying and selling stocks based on rumour and incidental developments are haphazard activities that generally add little or no value and, in the hands of inexperienced investors, lead to losses more often than not. Even stock-picking based on fundamental research adds minimal value compared to getting the asset mix right in the first place. The policies of most pension funds stipulate the fund should hold 50 to 70 per cent of the assets in equities and the balance in fixed-income securities and cash.

We have hinted strongly that equities should play a significant role for any investor with a long-term investment horizon. Returns from equities tend to beat bonds by a large margin when inflation and bond yields are low and rising, and more or less match bonds when inflation and bond yields are high and falling. If bond yields are getting set to rise for the next 20 or 30 years, which will lead to dismal results, why not invest 100 per cent in equities if retirement remains 10, 20, or more years away? One good reason is that the future is unknowable, and it may not unfold the way we expect. The best solution is to diversify investments and avoid the well-known risk of putting all your eggs in one basket.

That's the strategy followed by large pension funds with hundreds of millions of dollars in assets. Those funds are managed by a small army of professional investment advisors and the corporate sponsor has a greater capacity to cope with risk than any individual investor. If these funds invest 30 to 50 per cent in government and corporate bonds—and they do—the more vulnerable individual investor needs to think twice about following a different path.

Invest, Don't Gamble

Saving for retirement is a serious business. Even if you are highly confident that equities will outperform bonds over your investment horizon and decided to place every dollar in equities, are you up to the stress involved if and when the market suffers a severe downturn? Probably not. Remember, this is an investment, not a gamble. For most of us, the risk is not worth the anxiety we are likely to face. It's a well-known fact in both psychology and investing that the stress we feel about losses exceeds the joy we feel when we experience a comparable gain. We all tend to enjoy good news less than we suffer from bad news.

How should we choose the asset mix then? Figure 13.4 shows real returns averaged over 25-year periods for three different proportions of equities and bonds. As the graph suggests, the asset mix wouldn't have made much difference since 1990 or so, because equities and bonds have performed about the same since then. Before 1990, the 70/30 mix (70 per cent equities) was superior by a significant margin, and the 30/70 mix was clearly the worst. An investor choosing a 30/70 mix would typically be more risk-averse, yet such a person was exposed to more long-term risk than the 70/30 investor. If our assessment of the outlook for bonds is correct, the last five years may be the closest that a 30/70 bond portfolio comes to overtaking a 70/30 portfolio for a long time to come. The 70/30 portfolio is a better bet for the foreseeable future.

Figure 13.4: How Long-Term Returns Vary by Asset Mix

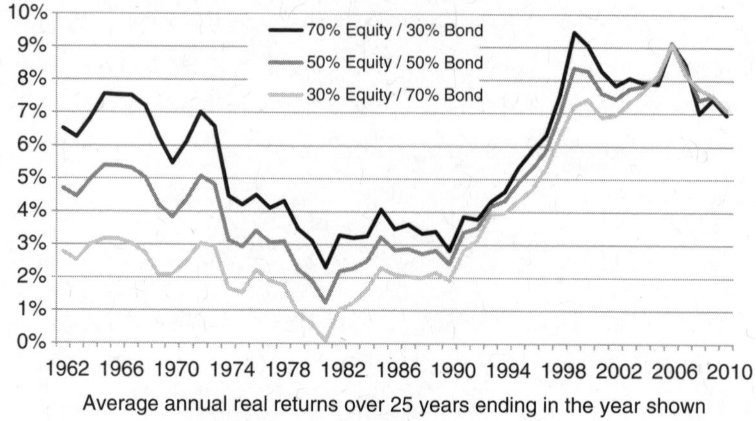

Average annual real returns over 25 years ending in the year shown

We freely admit that investing 70 per cent in equities would be regarded as risky given the skittishness of investors worldwide. The more risk-averse investors might want to consider a lesser exposure to equities, but they need to know that any low-risk investment these days is not even keeping up with inflation.

14

Managing Your Portfolio

Depending on the assets you have in your RRSP, you will have a number of options for managing your investments. If you have less than $500,000, you will probably invest in mutual funds or in ETFs (see investment terms just below). If your assets exceed $500,000, you can gain access to the full services of an investment-counselling firm, which can offer you pooled funds at much lower ongoing management fees than mutual funds. The investment-counselling firm will also help you to establish your asset mix at no extra charge. If you are lucky enough to build your assets up to the $2 million range, the investment-counselling firm may offer more services within the same fee envelope, such as estate planning and cash flow management. These thresholds are approximate and will vary from one investment firm to another.

In some cases, your employer will give you the option of putting your personal RRSP monies in the same investment vehicles that are offered under the employer's defined contribution pension plan or group RRSP. If so, you should seriously consider exercising that option. The investment fees will almost certainly be much lower than what you are paying in a mutual fund which means your investment returns after fees should outperform mutual fund returns.

Nevertheless, take a close look at the fees and the choice of invest-ment options before committing yourself.

If you have less than $500,000 in an RRSP and you are not a sophisticated investor, you can get investment advice by going through a bank branch and enlisting the services of a financial plan-ner. The financial planner gets paid by the mutual fund companies when the planner directs your monies to mutual funds.

You don't have to go through a planner or an investment-counselling firm. If you are savvy enough, you can simply set up an RRSP account with a discount broker and use your RRSP assets to buy ETFs or mutual funds. You will also have the option of choosing your own individual stocks and bonds, but this is not recommended unless (a) you have more than $250,000, which is the minimum amount needed to allow you to diversify your investments, and (b) you know what you are doing!

SOME USEFUL INVESTMENT TERMS

A *mutual fund* is a fund in which the assets of many investors are pooled for the purpose of keeping investment manage-ment costs down. Mutual funds are regulated by a securities commission and must provide a prospectus that sets out the rules and risks of the fund.

A mutual fund is a type of *pooled fund*. This is both a generic term and the phrase often used to refer to funds offered by investment management firms to pension funds, endowment funds, and sophisticated investors. Because a prospectus is not needed in these cases and because pooled funds are sold through a different distribution channel, the management fees are usually much lower than for a mutual fund.

A mutual fund or a pooled fund can be invested solely in equities *(equity fund)* or bonds *(bond fund)* or both equities and bonds *(balanced fund)*. Mutual funds and pooled funds can be bought or sold at the price that prevails at the end of each trading day.

Like mutual funds, *equity-traded funds* or ETFs hold a basket of securities. One key difference is that ETFs can be bought and sold at any time in the trading day (rather than at the end of the day) just like stocks or bonds. This is possible because ETFs are closed whereas mutual funds are usually open, meaning they can take in more money at any time to add more units. Another difference is that ETFs usually track an index such as the S&P/TSX or a sub-index such as the S&P/TSX Financials Index. This means ETFs are *passive* investments. Mutual funds can also be passively managed to mimic an index, but more typically they are *actively* managed. The biggest difference between them is in fees. The typical fee for a Canadian ETF is about 20 basis points. The fee for an actively managed mutual fund can be 250 basis points or more.

A *basis point* is one hundredth of a percentage point. For example, an investment management fee of 1 per cent of assets would be expressed as 100 basis points or 100 bps for short.

Choosing an Investment Manager

Before you choose your investment manager, decide whether you want to invest your money in (passive) index funds, active funds, or a combination of both. A passive manager tries to track the performance of a given index such as the S&P/TSX (a Canadian benchmark index) or the S&P 500 (an American index). An active manager selects the securities with the intention of trying to beat the index. Because tracking an index is fairly straightforward, passive management is usually less expensive than active. Fees for a major Canadian index equity fund can be less than 20 basis points; for major U.S. index funds, the fees can be even lower. The theoretical drawback to index funds is that they will simply mirror the market, not beat it, which is something an active manager is supposed to be able to do. Consistently outperforming the index, however, is not as easy as it sounds.

Actively managed funds rely on the skills and knowledge of a management team. It's a little like choosing between taking a bus to your destination or driving your own car. The bus is cheaper, but it can't deviate from the route and visit friends along the way. Managers of actively managed funds have to believe they can exceed the returns generated by indexed funds, choosing the winners and dumping the losers according to the profits that can be earned. This, of course, comes at a price. The annual fee to participate in an actively managed mutual fund is generally 200 to 300 basis points (2 to 3 per cent of your assets), while an actively managed bond mutual fund might charge 150 to 200 basis points.

If you choose active management, you will want your manager to do better than just beat the market index; he or she must outperform the market after deducting the investment fees. For example, if the S&P/TSX climbs 7 per cent in a given year, and the fee for your Canadian equity fund is 2.5 per cent, your equity fund manager should be expected to generate a return of at least 9.5 per cent—otherwise, you may as well have placed your monies in an index fund.

Can active management outperform the appropriate index fund on a regular basis? Not as often as you may hope or expect. If you ask investment experts who consults to major pension funds, they will probably not give you a straight answer on this question, although they might say that active management *should* do better than an index at least during down markets. When actuaries need to make long-term forecasts of the returns for an actively managed pension fund, the Canadian Institute of Actuaries instructs them to ignore the possibility that the manager will beat the index (after fees) unless they can prove the manager has done so consistently in the past.

The vast majority of Canadian pension plans invest their monies with an active manager, but this doesn't necessarily mean you should as well. A large pension plan is paying management fees of only 30 or 40 basis points, and a very large plan might be paying even less, so the overall cost for active management in these cases is almost negligible. You, however, need to decide if it is worth your while to pay 200 to 300 basis points for active management.

Fees Are Important

The importance of fees cannot be emphasized enough, because small differences add up to significant differences in real dollars over the life of your investment. For example, assume you have been saving 8 per cent of your salary over 30 years, and your current pay level is now $100,000. Let's also assume that you were invested exclusively in an equity fund that matched the return of the S&P/TSX Composite, the main Canadian equity index. If annual management fees for the fund were 40 basis points, which is what you might expect from an index fund available to retail investors, your account balance after 30 years would be about $453,000. If annual management fees were 250 basis points, which is typical for an active manager, the account balance would be just $316,000.

Remember that active management is supposed to add value, so make sure it does. If you are invested in an actively managed fund, whether it is a pooled fund or a mutual fund, know how much you are paying for fund management, and whether the fund's performance consistently beats a comparable index by a sufficient margin to justify the fee.

Manager Selection Process

Many guidelines exist for selecting an active fund manager, whether it is a mutual fund or an investment-counselling firm. Here is the process that investment consultants within actuarial firms use to assist pension plan sponsors in selecting an investment manager.

Identifying the Universe

"Universe" in this context refers to the array of potential fund managers that might be suitable choices for your portfolio. The eVestment Alliance investment database for institutional balanced funds lists nearly 100 funds.

Applying a Filter

We want to reduce the list to a manageable size for easier analysis. This involves applying some criteria that will filter out less suitable choices. Possible criteria include batting average, information ratio, and upside/downside capture.

- *Batting average* is the ratio of times that a manager's performance exceeds that of the index, based on monthly data, spanning 10 years where available. The greater the number of data points, the higher the degree of confidence that the results are valid (meaning that they are the product of skill rather than luck). The top performers typically have a long-term batting average from the high .500s to the low .600s, meaning they beat the index about 60 per cent of the time.

- *Information ratio* takes batting average a step further to look at consistency and relative volatility. Managers whose record of outperformance consists of relatively few instances of abnormally high returns are more likely to be exhibiting luck rather than skill.

- *Upside/downside capture* ratio measures the relative percentage gain of a fund compared to the benchmark when markets are positive. It also measures the percentage loss relative to the benchmark when markets are negative. Ideally, a fund should capture more than the benchmark's gains and less than the benchmark's losses. Thus, a score greater than 100 per cent in upside capture and less than 100 per cent in downside capture is preferred.

Analyzing Time Series

Each fund is sorted against the three metrics described above for 10 discrete time periods. For example, all funds with 10 years of history are ranked according to their batting average. The exercise is then repeated for all funds with nine years of history and so on. Funds that appear in the top quartile of each time series seven out of the 10 times make it onto a short list representing funds that consistently performed well over multiple time periods for a particular metric.

Weeding Out Specialty, Closed, and Non-Pooled Funds

Some funds that make it onto the screened list are anomalies that were misclassified or are extreme in their asset allocation. These funds are removed from consideration, along with funds that may have recently been closed to new clients. Finally, any remaining funds not offered on a pooled basis are removed.

Performing a Qualitative Review

Having applied the filter to reduce the number of candidates to a manageable size, the next step is to conduct a qualitative review. Recently acquired fund management companies and those that experienced significant turnover of key personnel are excluded. Also excluded are managers whose typical mandate is very different from your own mandate. A manager is going to be more attuned to the client's needs if he or she has at least several other clients with similar needs and portfolios of comparable size.

Adapting the Process

Let's face it: the process just described is over-the-top for the average investor. You will need to adapt it to your own situation and apply the steps that are within your means. If you are doing this alone, you can meet with several respectable managers. You might ask them questions that relate to batting average and information ratio and maybe dispense with upside/downside capture. If you are using a financial advisor to help you select your investment manager, you can ask the advisor to apply these tests.

If you have a large enough portfolio to be dealing directly with an investment-counselling firm, meeting with the firm is an important part of the selection process. You want to be sure you will have a comfort level with the service representative who will act as a main liaison, not necessarily with the salesperson trying to land you as a client. Ask to see examples of the reports you would receive periodically on the status of your investments.

You need to understand the reports and be confident that they provide you with useful information. Also, look at the statement of investment policy your manager will draft for you, showing your target asset mix and the amount of discretion the manager has to deviate from the long-term mix. Consider restricting the freedom to alter the long-term mix at least until you are comfortable with the manager. Does the manager provide modelling tools so you can determine how much you should be saving to meet your retirement goal? Finally, never forget about fees. Ask how much they will be, and how and when they will be applied. While this process is a sound one, please note that it will not guarantee above-average performance. There are no guarantees in the investment world.

Monitoring

If your monies are actively managed by an investment-counselling firm, you should be meeting once or twice a year with a representative of the firm (an investment counsellor). If your monies are in a mutual fund, the meeting might take place with the financial planner who placed you into those funds. The purpose of these meetings is to review recent fund performance as well as to learn of any changes in key personnel among the people who manage the funds. These meetings should also entail a review of the asset mix, whether any changes in mix took place, or whether any changes are advisable. You will also want to know the manager's outlook for the capital markets in the short term and any changes he or she might suggest in the asset mix.

It should be a two-way communication. Be sure to tell your financial planner or investment counsellor of any changes in your situation, such as a change in marital status, whether you have delayed your proposed retirement date, or if you have decided to purchase an annuity at retirement rather than transferring your assets to a Registered Retirement Income Fund (RRIF).

If you are working with an investment-counselling firm, you may have some flexibility in the kind of reports you can receive. Tell your manager to keep the reports fairly simple and make sure you understand them. Complex reports that will never be read, much less absorbed, are a waste of everyone's time. What makes reports most useful is if they show the type of information that helps you assess your manager's performance objectively, rather than the information the investment-counselling firm wants you to see. One of the more revealing things these reports can provide is a comparison of the manager's returns versus various market indices. For example, how does your U.S. equity fund (if you have one) compare with the S&P 500 Index over the same period? A long explanation as to why your manager failed to beat an index is not very useful. You are looking for results rather than excuses. One thing you should not do is compare your overall return to what your friends achieved with their manager. This simply isn't fair if their portfolio had a different asset mix.

Statement of Investment Policy

Whether your fund assets are actively or passively managed, you should have a statement of investment policies and principles (SIP&P). The SIP&P describes your tolerance for risk (high, medium, low); your investment horizon (how many years until you plan to retire); and your long-term asset mix target (bonds versus equities). If you have retained an investment-counselling firm, they will work with you to produce an SIP&P at no extra charge. If you have a financial planner, he or she also should be doing this for you. The SIP&P should also establish ranges for each asset class, which means specifying how far the manager can deviate from the long-term asset mix target. For example, if the asset mix target was to invest 60 per cent in equities and 40 per cent in bonds, the range might fix the minimum investment in equities at 50 per cent and the maximum at 70 per cent. There is some merit in keeping the ranges fairly narrow, which means restricting the amount of discretion your manager has. This reduces the tendency to be overexposed to an asset class (such as Canadian equities) at the peak of the market or underexposed at the bottom. Narrow ranges also force more frequent rebalancing of your asset mix, which actuaries suggest gives you a little added return over the long run.

Think Twice Before Changing Your Asset Mix

Having chosen the asset mix that best matches your risk profile and your long-term goals, should you ever vary the mix? Generally, we suggest not changing the mix, especially in reaction to ups and downs in the stock market. Remember, the future is unknowable. Market timing has been proven almost impossible to execute successfully and consistently over time. It is difficult not to succumb to greed at the top of the market, or to fear at the bottom, and both of these emotions encourage us to change our mix in the wrong direction.

Nevertheless, there are times when changing your mix can make sense. One instance is when your investment horizon changes significantly, which it will do over time. You should be reducing the equity weighting in your portfolio as you age in order to reduce the volatility of the fund's performance as you approach retirement. Some investment managers make this process easy by enrolling you in target date funds, which modify your asset mix automatically.

Another exception may occur when yields on bonds are at historic highs or lows. Over long periods, fixed-income markets are more predictable than equity markets, especially when yields appear to have only one direction in which to move, such as is currently the case.

It might also be prudent to change your mix when you are invested fairly aggressively in equities, the markets have been buoyant, and you are ahead of your goal of accumulating retirement savings. If you can now reach your original retirement goal with a less aggressive mix, reducing the chances of disaster in the process, it may be worth considering.

Even if you have no intention of changing your asset mix, it will drift on its own over time if left unattended. That is because one asset class will typically do better than another, which means your exposure to that asset class will rise in proportion to the total fund. It is the job of your financial advisor or investment counsellor to ensure your asset mix stays within a given range. Actuaries have determined that regularly rebalancing your mix provides a lift to your long-term returns in the order of 25 to 50 basis points per annum (0.25 to 0.5 per cent). This little bonus comes at virtually no cost and with no additional risk. For this reason, it is important to rebalance the portfolio from time to time, and to maintain the desired long-term asset mix.

15

Your Expected Return

Most Canadians don't begin to take retirement seriously until they are at least in their thirties, and more likely in their forties. And those are the responsible ones! This leaves them with perhaps 20 or 30 years to build the assets they'll need when their full-time working years are over. If you are using capital accumulation vehicles such as RRSPs to build your retirement security, the key to success is in knowing what return you can expect on your savings. This will dictate how much you should save and when you can afford to retire.

The future is unknowable in many respects, but a number of indicators will give us at least an inkling of the kind of investment return we can expect in the next 20 to 30 years. For example, in 1975 inflation and interest rates were high and climbing, and the economy was still struggling to cope with the first of the oil-price shocks. In spite of all that, we would have had reason to believe that the years 1975 to 1999 would turn out better for investors than the period between 1951 and 1975. One indicator was the level of inflation at the start of the period and its most likely future direction. The principle of reversion to the mean suggests that when a given indicator (like inflation) strays too far from historic norms, it usually snaps back. Inflation was at a very low level in the 1950s, generally in the 0 to 2 per cent range, but then started climbing in the 1960s. By 1975, it was approaching double digits. Reversion to the mean suggested it would eventually return to low single digits, which is precisely what happened, although it took a while.

Rising inflation is positively deadly for the government bond market. From 1951 to 1975, long-term bonds produced an average nominal return of just 2.7 per cent per annum, while inflation averaged 3.4 per cent, so bonds lost ground over a 25-year period. Rising inflation is not especially favourable to stocks either but stocks can still do reasonably well. Over the same 25-year period, Canadian stocks had a nominal return of 8.9 per cent and U.S. stocks did even better at 10.1 per cent (measured in Canadian dollars for comparability).

The trend reversed direction from 1975 to 1999. Inflation in the mid-1970s had reached almost 10 per cent, rose even higher into the early 1980s, and then began a long gradual slide to about 2 per cent in the late 1990s. As inflation declined, so did bond yields, which meant that bond prices rose (remember that lower interest rates produce higher bond prices).

All this does not bode well for investing in bonds today because current inflation rates and bond yields resemble the early 1950s much more than the mid-1970s. Yields on long-term Government of Canada bonds are currently the lowest they have been since records were first kept. If higher inflation returns, yields will rise, but they are likely to rise even if inflation remains low, because the current low yields are a global response to a rare financial crisis that has lingered for years. Rising yields will translate into lower bond prices and capital losses that may swamp any interest income the bonds pay out.

The only scenario under which bonds might do well is if yields fall still further. This can only happen, however, if we experience a bout of deflation, which is defined as the situation when consumer prices actually drop for a prolonged period of time. At first blush, lower prices sound attractive, but the effects of deflation are disastrous for economies and equity investments. Pensioners drawing income from defined benefit pension plans do better, assuming the plan sponsor can keep the plan fully funded in a deflationary environment, but almost everyone else does worse. Deflation occurred in Canada and the U.S. during the 1930s, and has afflicted Japan since the early 1990s. One of its effects is reduced economic growth, leading to high unemployment. Once an economy is in this state, it is hard to break out of it, as Japan has been learning.

We don't anticipate deflation, but investment managers will still be hard pressed to produce decent returns in this low-yield environment.

Building Blocks to Estimate Future Growth

In the remainder of this chapter, we will develop a realistic forecast of the investment return you can expect over the longer term. To do so, we will use the same building-block approach that actuaries use when they set the discount rate to perform pension plan valuations. The building-block approach involves breaking the problem into smaller problems for easier analysis. Basically, we will estimate the future inflation rate, the real return over inflation from the main asset classes, the deduction for fees, and the overall return for different asset mixes.

Inflation

The performance of various asset classes is usually measured in terms of real returns, that is to say, the investment return they can achieve in excess of inflation. Investors tend to think in terms of overall return including inflation (the nominal return). To arrive at the nominal return, we need to estimate the future inflation rate and add it to the weighted real return on each asset class.

Over the 90-year period for which there is a statistical record for the Canadian Consumer Price Index (CPI), the average annual change in prices was 2.9 per cent. We can use this as a reliable approximation . of the inflation rate to expect over the next 25 years.

Figure 15.1: Changes in Canada's CPI since 1924

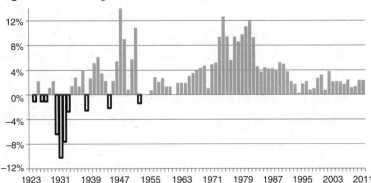

We could fine-tune Figure 5.1 by taking into account the Bank of Canada's policy of limiting inflation to between 1 and 3 per cent annually. Indeed, inflation has floated in the 2 per cent range in Canada for about 20 years now. While there is no guarantee the government will stick to this policy, we at least have a reasonable argument for inflation to stay under control over the long term and to remain somewhat below its 90-year average. Based on this data, actuaries generally assume inflation in Canada will range from 2 to 2.5 per cent, which makes 2.25 per cent the midpoint.

Can inflation move higher than 2.25 per cent? It certainly can. When forecasting any future development, we all tend to be heavily influenced by current conditions. Back in the early 1980s, it was common for forecasters to assume that long-term inflation would remain at 9 per cent or higher. Similarly, while no one is expecting high inflation any time soon, it is possible that the last four years of quantitative easing will eventually lead to runaway inflation.

The Return on Fixed-Income Investments

The term "fixed income" usually refers to bonds, but it also includes mortgages and guaranteed investment certificates (GICs). The fixed-income return over the next 25 years will depend heavily on current yields. If yields stay consistently low, returns will be low. If yields go up appreciably, returns may even be negative because rising yields mean lower bond prices. Either way, the result is likely to be fairly low returns for many years to come.

Yields depend heavily on inflation expectations, which are currently almost non-existent. Yields also depend on the credit rating of the issuer. The Government of Canada boasts the highest rating, followed in order by the provinces and blue-chip corporations. The other factor affecting yields is the term of the bond: longer-term bonds usually deliver a higher yield. All high-quality bonds currently have very low yields, so the only significant return one can expect is from capital gains. This requires yields to fall even lower, which is next to impossible.

Over the last century, most of the 25-year periods that started with low inflation and low yields occurred in the 1930s, 1940s, and 1950s. During these periods, the nominal annual return on long-term Canada bonds averaged between 2.5 and 3.5 per cent. The real return averaged between 0 and 1 per cent, and even dropped into negative territory for many years.

Against this background, actuaries estimate that real returns on bonds over the next 25 years will average between 1 and 1.6 per cent depending on the term of the bond. The only surprising aspect of this forecast is its optimism. The annual real return on long-term government bonds over the 30 years ending in 1981 was actually negative 1.3 per cent. The one reason to expect bonds to fare a little better is if one assumes that some of the bond portfolio is going to be invested in high-yield bonds. With all these considerations in mind, we think it is reasonable to assume a real return on fixed-income investments of 1.25 per cent annually—but caution that this may prove optimistic.

The Return on Equities

In their building-block approach to estimating returns, actuaries vary their expected return on equities according to the specific sub-class of equities. At the moment, they assume 5 to 5.25 per cent to be their best estimate of the real return on Canadian and U.S. equities, and 6 per cent or better on international equities. Unfortunately, international equities usually carry both a higher management fee and greater risk factor; both eat into the additional return they are expected to deliver. For the sake of simplicity, we'll assume both Canadian and U.S. equities will produce a real return of 5.25 per cent, and ignore the possibly higher returns from international equities.

Why are we assuming the real return on equities will be just 5.25 per cent when over the long term it has averaged closer to 7 per cent? While something closer to 7 per cent is still possible, a couple of facts argue for lower returns. One is that bonds and equities are competing asset classes. If companies trying to raise money are paying less interest on fixed-income debt than on equity, why would they raise money in the stock market? The same factors that conspire to keep bond yields low may also have a dampening effect on equity returns, a situation that has not always been true, but should be acknowledged. The better reason to expect the lower figure is that an aging population will mean lower GDP growth. Slower economic growth will translate into slower profit growth producing, in turn, slower growth in dividends and slower growth in stock prices.

Rebalancing and Diversification

Without getting into the technical details, actuaries believe that returns can be enhanced by up to 50 basis points through diversification and regular rebalancing of the portfolio. Here, we will somewhat arbitrarily assume that this process adds 40 basis points.

Evaluating Fees

As mentioned earlier, the annual investment management fee can range from 10 basis points to more than 300 basis points depending on the asset class and whether the assets are actively managed. Given the lack of hard evidence that active management adds value, most actuaries assume that the extra return generated by active management is no greater than the management fee itself. We will assume that assets are invested passively in index funds with a management fee of 50 basis points including custodial costs.

The Result

Putting all the building blocks together, Table15.1 shows the expected nominal investment return on an annual basis. Note that to calculate the real return, we subtracted the expected inflation rate of 2.25 per cent.

Table 15.1: Nominal and Real Return by Asset Mix

	Asset Mix (Equity/Bond)		
	30/70	50/50	70/30
Expected nominal return net of fees	4.6 per cent	5.4 per cent	6.2 per cent
Expected real return net of fees	2.35 per cent	3.15 per cent	3.95 per cent

These figures are rather sobering and at least a little depressing. With bond yields so low, one pays a high price these days for having an asset mix heavily weighted in bonds. A nominal annual return of 4.6 per cent over the long term sounds dismal by any measure, and even the 6.2 per cent produced by an aggressive asset mix is much less than investors have grown accustomed to expect. Still, this is the range of returns that actuaries are assuming these days when making their forecasts.

To offer a glimmer of hope, the return may eventually prove to be higher because equities could do better than the assumed 5.25 per cent for the reasons mentioned earlier, even if few actuaries are willing to bet on it. On the other hand, bond returns may be even lower than the 1.25 per cent we have assumed.

In our projections of RRSP balances in Chapters 10, 11, and 12, we assumed a total fund return of 5.75 per cent after investment fees. This implicitly assumes that investors begin with a 70 per cent equity/30 per cent bond mix when retirement is still some years off, and then move to a more conservative 50/50 mix as they approach retirement.

16

Choosing Your Savings Vehicle

Unless you participate in a workplace pension plan, you will need to choose a vehicle to hold the investments that will help fund your retirement income. So far, we have been assuming that the funding vehicle will be an RRSP, though that isn't necessarily the case. While an RRSP is by far the most common choice during the accumulation phase, there are several other possibilities, depending on whether you have access to an employer-sponsored plan. (Appendix D summarizes the features of various tax-assisted retirement vehicles.)

You have a number of savings vehicles to choose from, and the best one for your specific needs is not always obvious. The following discussion gives some guidance.

Why Invest in a Tax-Assisted Vehicle?

The biggest drag on an investment portfolio is paying tax. A tax-assisted vehicle reduces that drag because the investment income is not taxed during the accumulation phase. Tax-deferral is valuable because it enables you to earn investment income on monies that would otherwise have been taxed away. This can make a major difference over the long periods of time needed to build retirement assets. For example, if you invest $10,000 at 6 per cent annual interest and do not pay tax on the earnings, your balance will be $32,000 after 20 years. If the same earnings were not tax-sheltered and were subject to a marginal tax rate of 46 per cent, you will have only $21,900.

"Tax-assisted" can also mean you receive a tax deduction when you make a contribution to the vehicle. This tax deduction is one of the most attractive features of RRSPs. To continue the previous example, if you made a one-time contribution of $10,000 to an RRSP and earned 6 per cent annually on the money, you would have both the $32,000 balance after 20 years plus another $4,600 in the form of a tax refund (46 per cent of the RRSP-eligible $10,000).

You eventually have to pay for the tax break, of course. Since you receive a tax deduction when the money goes into the RRSP, you have to pay tax when you withdraw it. In spite of this, you are almost always better off investing in an RRSP or other tax-assisted vehicle rather than investing outside of one. There are exceptions, though.

One exception is in the case of low-income workers who would lose some or all of their Guaranteed Income Supplement in retirement when they convert their RRSP savings into income. Another exception is if your marginal tax rate is higher after retirement than it was when you contributed to the RRSP. If so, you could be better off investing outside the RRSP and paying tax as the investment income was realized. The immediate tax deduction for the RRSP contribution might not be worth as much as the eventual income tax you pay in retirement, when your RRSP savings are converted into income. Moreover, you don't enjoy the favourable tax treatment that applies to dividends and capital gains outside of an RRSP. Dividends and capital gains that are earned inside an RRSP are taxed at the same rate as ordinary income when the monies are withdrawn.

Another exception: real estate. After the financial crisis of 2008–2009, many investors shied away from stocks and bonds, choosing to buy real estate either as a vacation property or as an investment property to be rented out. Investing in your principal residence is an especially effective option in Canada because no tax applies as your home appreciates in value, and any capital gain is free of income tax when you sell. It has actually been advantageous to overbuy a family home, then downsize at retirement to maximize the gain. Of course, this only works if house prices rise strongly over the period. Despite or maybe because of the robust housing market seen in recent years, this is not a certainty going forward.

Even if your real estate investment is not your principal residence, it's best to hold real estate outside an RRSP. Any appreciation on the investment will not be taxed immediately even outside the RRSP. As mentioned earlier, capital gains will be fully taxed when withdrawn from the RRSP but only 50 per cent of the capital gains will be taxed (upon disposition) if the investment is held outside a registered plan.

The Accumulation Phase—RRSP or TFSA?

Retirement savings involve two phases: the accumulation (or savings) phase which ends at the point of retirement, and the de-accumulation (or payout) phase which takes place throughout retirement. We will start with the accumulation phase, which is where we find RRSPs and TFSAs.

RRSPs were introduced in 1957 and, after a slow start, became the retirement savings vehicle of choice for anyone who was not covered by a workplace pension plan. Contributions to RRSPs are tax-deductible, which means you will receive a tax refund when you file your tax return after year-end. The investment income within the RRSP is not taxed during the accumulation phase, but you will be taxed on any withdrawals of assets, either before or after retirement. You can only keep your monies in an RRSP until age 71 at which time you need to transfer them to one of the de-accumulation vehicles described later in this chapter. As mentioned earlier, however, you may sometimes be better off saving outside of an RRSP even if the investments are not tax-assisted. Any time you are better off outside of an RRSP, you will find Tax-Free Savings Accounts (TFSAs) to be particularly advantageous.

The introduction of TFSAs in 2009 gave Canadians an alternative to saving in an RRSP. You do not receive a tax-deduction for the contribution going into the TFSA, but the upside is that the investment income is never taxed. And when you eventually take money out of the TFSA, the withdrawals are not subject to income tax. You can continue to deposit new monies (up to the allowable limit) into a TFSA as long as you want and you are not required to transfer the monies out at age 71 as is the case with an RRSP. In other words, a TFSA is both an accumulation and a de-accumulation vehicle. Thus, seniors can continue to build their TFSA tax shelter even while they must draw down their RRIF.

If you believe you will have a higher marginal tax rate in retirement than while you were working you are better off investing in a TFSA rather than an RRSP.[1] Hence, it may make sense for young people to be contributing to a TFSA instead of an RRSP early in their careers, a time when they are not yet in a high tax bracket.

In addition, if you expect your retirement income will be low enough that you will qualify to receive the Guaranteed Income Supplement (GIS), a TFSA is a *much* better choice than an RRSP. Unlike withdrawals from a RRIF or LIF (these are described later in this chapter), money from a TFSA in retirement does not count as income for GIS purposes, so it does not reduce your entitlement to the GIS. By contrast, if you are married and retired, every $4 withdrawn from a RRIF or LIF will reduce your GIS entitlement by $1. If you are not married, your GIS will be reduced by $1 for every $2 of RRIF or LIF income.

Canadians in the top income-tax bracket would be better off maxing out their RRSP contributions before investing in a TFSA because the tax deductions for the RRSP contributions are worth more to them.

DC Pension Plan or RRSP?

You might have the choice of participating in your employer's defined contribution (DC) pension plan, if it sponsors one, or investing in your own RRSP. The best route to follow? If contributions to your employer's DC plan are matched in whole or in part by your employer, you should max out on those contributions before putting money into your own RRSP. It's the easiest and most logical way to increase your retirement savings. Don't be concerned about any future financial troubles your employer may encounter because money in a DC plan is held separately from the employer's assets and cannot be touched by creditors.

If your employer's DC plan permits you to make additional voluntary contributions that the employer does not match, the decision is a little more difficult, but you are usually better off making additional contributions through the employer's DC plan than your own RRSP. That is because you will escape paying administration fees under the DC plan and investment management fees are probably much lower under the DC plan than in your RRSP. Check to confirm this is the case before making a decision, however; some small DC pension plans are charged high management fees. Finally, additional voluntary contributions to the DC plan are not subject to locking-in, providing you with some flexibility if you need it in the future.

You may also have a locked-in RRSP or Locked-in Retirement Account (LIRA) if you participated in a workplace pension plan and transferred the monies out of that plan when you left your employer. In a locked-in RRSP or LIRA, some additional restrictions apply at retirement, such as rules regarding allowable survivor benefits and unisex annuity rates.

The De-Accumulation Phase—RRIFs

In the de-accumulation phase, you start to reap the rewards of all those years of saving. If your savings vehicle was an RRSP, note that you cannot receive income directly from an RRSP in retirement. At the point of retirement you have a choice to make: you must either transfer your RRSP assets to a Registered Retirement Income Fund (RRIF) and manage the assets inside the RRIF as you did with your RRSP, or transfer the money to an insurance company for the purchase of an annuity. In neither case is the money taxed as a result of the transfer, so the tax treatment should not concern you.

A RRIF operates much like an RRSP in the sense that you control the investments and the investment income is tax-sheltered as long as the monies remain in the plan. It is the opposite of an RRSP in the sense that you can draw income from a RRIF but cannot contribute to one. While there is no maximum on the amount you can withdraw from a RRIF in a given year, the amount withdrawn is subject to a minimum that varies by age. You don't have to transfer your money from your RRSP to a RRIF until age 71, but if you transfer it earlier than 71, you must withdraw the minimum percentages of your RRIF assets as shown in Table 16.1.

Table 16.1: Minimum Withdrawal Percentages from a RRIF

Age at Start of Year	RRIFs Set Up After 1992	Age at Start of Year	RRIFs Set Up After 1992
65	4.00%	80	8.75%
66	4.17%	81	8.99%
67	4.35%	82	9.27%
68	4.55%	83	9.58%
69	4.76%	84	9.93%
70	5.00%	85	10.33%
71	7.38%	86	10.79%
72	7.48%	87	11.33%
73	7.59%	88	11.96%
74	7.71%	89	12.71%
75	7.85%	90	13.62%
76	7.99%	91	14.73%
77	8.15%	92	16.12%
78	8.33%	93	17.92%
79	8.53%	94+	20.00%

Note the big jump in the size of the minimum RRIF payout at age 71, from 5 to 7.38 per cent. The reason the government wants to see high withdrawals is that the RRIF income is subject to taxation and the government is always hungry for tax revenue. The high minimums have been a major source of contention among retirees who feel they are being forced to deplete their RRIF faster than they would like to do. It feeds on widespread fears that they will outlive their assets, a phenomenon we have coined "depletion anxiety." This is described in the next section.

Besides RRIFs, there are also LIFs (Life Income Funds) and LRIFs (Locked-in Retirement Income Funds). LIFs and LRIFs are similar to RRIFs, except that the monies that are transferred into them originally came from registered pension plans and are subject to some further restrictions.

Depletion Anxiety

It's normal to want to live a long life, assuming that one enjoys good health. The darker side of a long life is the fear that it gives rise to: what if you outlive your money? Next to health concerns, this is the biggest fear we have in retirement, one that is acknowledged by 62 per cent of Canadians, according to a survey by the Canadian Institute of Actuaries.

The fear of not having enough money is common even among very wealthy people, who according to the Boston College study mentioned earlier felt that their assets needed to be about 25 per cent higher on average for them to feel truly financially secure—even though their assets totalled at least $25 million already!

By the time you are on the cusp of retirement, you have probably calculated how much money you will need to generate sufficient income for the rest of your life. You have probably even added in some margins in that calculation just to be extra sure. When the decision is upon you, however, it's difficult to pull the trigger. When you start drawing down your savings, it suddenly hits you that the one pile of assets that separates you from near-poverty is being eroded away, and as it does so, it is natural to be afraid that it will run out too quickly.

For people who have not saved enough for retirement, depletion anxiety is a valid concern. For many others, however, the fear is more perceived than real. Even when some pre-retirees have built in an ample cushion to cover every contingency they can think of, from stock market crashes and poor health to cuts in government pensions and runaway inflation, depletion anxiety persists. What if they missed something?

Annuities: The Cure for Depletion Anxiety

The easiest way to reduce the fear of outliving your savings is to purchase an annuity upon retirement. Annuities are sold and backed by insurance companies, and no one in Canada has ever lost a dollar because an insurance company went under. In the highly unlikely event that the insurance company holding your annuity cannot pay in full, your annuity would be guaranteed by Assuris up to $2,000 a month or 85 per cent of the monthly income, whichever is higher. If your annuity is greater than $2,000 a month, you can split the annuity purchase between two insurance companies and double the Assuris coverage.

The strange thing is that, as strong and pervasive as depletion anxiety is, very few people buy annuities. As described in the next chapter, there are many possible reasons for this, but most likely the central reason is that retirees are loath to give up control of their money. As long as the money is in a RRIF, retirees can manage it as they please and, in the event that they die early, the lump sum will form part of their estate. The need for control trumps fear!

Delaying C/QPP Payments

Another method of ensuring that a greater part of your retirement income will last your lifetime no matter how long you live is to delay receiving C/QPP payments until you reach 70 years of age. The longer you defer these payments, the larger the monthly benefit will be and the less that recipients have to worry about longevity risk.

By collecting C/QPP at age 70 instead of 65, the amount payable will be 42 per cent higher (or it will be by 2013 when the new rules are phased in), fully indexed and payable for life. Once again, few people have availed themselves of this option, even though it provides ironclad protection against depletion anxiety. About 40 per cent of plan contributors choose to receive their first CPP cheque at age 60, the earliest age possible, despite the 36 per cent penalty imposed versus commencement at 65. By comparison, less than 2 per cent of Canadians start their CPP at 70 or later.

For example, consider someone who has just retired at 62. Assume this individual has worked since he was 23 and always earned at least as much as the CPP earnings ceiling. That means he has had five years (the period between age 18 and 22) when he had no earnings for C/QPP purposes. At 65, the maximum period of low earnings that can be ignored when calculating the CPP is eight years[2] plus the years between 65 and 70. This is known as the "dropout period." This individual would receive the maximum C/QPP pension, whether he started his pension at 62, 65, or 70. Using the 2012 figures for C/QPP and rounding to the nearest $100, he would be entitled to a CPP pension of $12,000 a year starting at 65, but just $9,300 at age 62. If he waits until 70, the annual amount payable for life is $16,800.

So by starting C/QPP payments at 70 instead of 65, the individual in our example would receive $7,500 more each year over the rest of his life, plus inflationary increases. If he has enough RRIF assets, he could draw from his RRIF balance until age 70 to tide him over until C/QPP pension starts. This strategy enables one to worry less about one's investments and focus instead on enjoying retirement more fully.

This strategy is not advisable if you have reason to believe your life expectancy is shorter than normal, and may not be advisable if you had more years of low earnings than the dropout provision allows for. If you didn't enter the workforce until age 25 and retired at age

60, you would have had seven years of low or no earnings between 18 and 24 plus another five years between 61 and 65. Your C/QPP pension would be about $7,700 a year starting at 60, and $10,500 a year starting at 65, instead of the $12,000 we saw earlier. In this case, you might be better off starting your C/QPP pension at 60 after all.

In general, if waiting until 65 does not result in having more years of low earnings than the dropout rules allow, you benefit by deferring the start of your CPP pension until you reach 70, assuming you are in good health. The decision grows more complicated if you have too many years of reduced earnings, in which case you may want to call Service Canada and explain your situation.

OAS payments cannot be received before age 65, but starting in 2013 they can be deferred until age 70 with a higher amount payable. The actuarial increase applying to OAS will be just 7.2 per cent a year rather than the 8.4 per cent that applies to C/QPP between 65 and 70 but, if you don't need the money early, then why not wait until 70 before you start collecting?

Much has been written about the shortcomings of capital accumulation plans for retirement purposes due to investment risk, longevity risk, hidden fees, and advisors with vested interests. You can minimize the risks and uncertainties by making strategic decisions about when you start your C/QPP and OAS pensions.

17

Should You Buy an Annuity?

The previous chapter explained that a retiree has the choice of transferring his or her assets from an RRSP to a RRIF or buying an annuity. A RRIF allows the retiree to continue to have control over the investments, but this control comes at a price. While a RRIF provides a great deal of flexibility and gives one at least the chance of doing better, it requires one to have substantial knowledge of investments, investment products, and hidden fees. Also, the income under a RRIF can be highly variable and, depending on the investments, one can suffer an investment loss. Finally, the minimum withdrawal rules starting at age 71 can cause anxiety among seniors who are concerned about out-living their assets.

The Purpose of Annuities

This is where annuities come in. An annuity involves handing over your retirement savings to a life insurance company which then provides you with a fixed monthly payment for the rest of your life. While annuities lack the complete flexibility of RRIFs, they effectively solve virtually all of the drawbacks of RRIFs as described above. By buying an annuity, you are transferring the longevity risk to the insurance company. If you live longer than the insurance company expected when they priced the annuity, you come out ahead. On the other hand, if you die early, you might get less than you paid for. We say "might" because if this is really a concern, you can opt for a survivor benefit that pays your beneficiaries a substantial amount.

Given the problem of depletion anxiety described in the last chapter, overcoming longevity risk is a big deal. No one knows how long they will live, so, in the absence of an annuity, how can you determine how quickly you can draw down your savings in retirement without running out? One approach is to spend less and keep some money in reserve in case you live for a very long time. This is, in fact, what many retirees do. As we saw in Chapter 8 (the phases of retirement), under-spending in retirement is more common than spending one's savings too quickly. It is less than ideal because it means retirees are leaving a lot of money on the table when they die.

The beauty of annuities is that the longevity risk is transferred from someone who is ill-equipped to handle it (i.e., you) to an entity whose business it is to absorb the risk (i.e., the insurance company). The insurer pools your annuity with those of a large number of other individuals. Even if no one can accurately predict when an individual will die, the insurance actuaries can estimate fairly closely the rates of death at a specific age for a large group of annuitants. The result is that annuitants can dispose of their longevity risk, remove the anxiety of investing their money after retirement, and ensure there will be no large unspent sums after they have passed away.

Annuities also address the matter of investment risk. The annuitant does not have to know anything about investments, and the amount of the monthly payments is fixed, so there are no surprises no matter what happens to the stock market. The payments are extremely secure, given the reserves that the insurance companies are required to maintain and the additional backstop provided by Assuris. Payments will be made for life, even if you live past 100. Finally, you have a great deal of flexibility in tailoring the survivor benefits you would like to see paid to your designated beneficiaries.

Variable Annuities and Annuity Derivatives

Insurance companies are coming out with new products that address the biggest perceived drawback of annuities: their lack of flexibility. There is a rapidly growing market for variable annuities and annuity derivatives that have life annuity-like features. While Canadian sales figures are not yet available, the volume of new variable annuity sales in the U.S. in 2010 exceeded $100 billion a year. Variable annuity assets under management by insurance companies total about $1.4 trillion.

Variable annuities are popular in the U.S. because they allow individuals to invest in all sorts of funds with different asset mixes but still receive insurance against longevity risk. For instance, you can buy a variable annuity that invests in an aggressive equity fund and, for an additional fee, attach a minimum guaranteed return so you have upside potential if the equity fund does well while you also have protection against downside risk.

For a fee, you can also attach a "guaranteed income for life" component which works much like a life annuity but is triggered only if market returns are bad. Lifetime income guarantee riders are very popular within variable annuities. Over 96 per cent of variable annuities sold in the U.S. in 2004 and over 75 per cent of variable annuities sold in the first half of 2005 contained lifetime income guarantee riders.

The most popular kind of lifetime income guarantee rider is called a Guaranteed Lifetime Withdrawal Benefit, first introduced in

Canada by Manulife in 2007. This rider provides complete exposure to market returns for funds invested and provides the holder with a guaranteed monthly withdrawal payment for life that never declines over time, and is ratcheted up annually if their invested funds are doing well. The main selling point to variable annuities is that they provide a variety of options: they can give you the opportunity to benefit when market returns are high while still having downside protection when market returns are low. The catch is that they are highly engineered products with irregular risks and costs that are not well understood by the public.

Present-Day Annuity Market in Canada

In Canada, annuities are available from virtually all major life insurance providers. They can commence at any age and the price varies by age, sex, and health status. They are usually quoted and sold in $100,000 increments, meaning that they are only a viable option if one has $100,000 or more. The most common format is to pay a one-time premium up front and then receive monthly annuity payments for life. In a typical contract at current interest rates, a $100,000 premium for a 65-year-old female might purchase an annuity of $510 a month, assuming no survivor benefit.

Generally contracts are targeted at people between the ages of 55 and 80. The contracts often stipulate a guarantee period which is a period of time when annuity payments will continue to be made even if the annuitant has died; the typical guarantee period is five or 10 years, but it can be up to 25 years. Since healthier people with higher than average income tend to buy annuities, the life expectancy of annuity buyers is significantly higher than for the average population. This means that anyone with serious health issues should steer clear of them.

Taxation of Annuities

In Canada, annuities can be purchased using money from either tax-assisted retirement funds (such as RRSPs, Locked-in RRSPs, RRIFs, LRIFs, LIFs, or pension funds) or non-tax-assisted funds. In the former case, the annuity income is taxed as regular income in the year that the income is received. For annuities purchased out of non-tax-assisted funds, only the interest portion of the annuity payment is taxed and the tax treatment depends on whether the annuity is prescribed or non-prescribed. Since this chapter focuses on annuities that are funded by RRSPs, we will not go into prescribed annuities here.

In general, annuities will not change the tax structure of the initial source of funds. Funds enjoying tax-deferred status will maintain that status when placed in an annuity and funds not enjoying tax-deferred status will not gain such status by being placed in an annuity.

The Under-Annuitization Puzzle

Annuitizing seems like such an elegant solution to longevity risk. There is only one problem: very few people choose annuities over a RRIF. One reason is that no one wants to enrich the insurance companies at their expense and this fear is not completely illusory. Research on annuity prices in the U.S. in the 1970s, 1980s, and 1990s found that annuities, on balance, did not provide very good value in those periods. Annuity payments in that era generally returned only 80 to 90 per cent return of premiums paid, in present value terms, leaving 10 to 20 per cent for the insurance companies to cover operating expenses and take a profit.

In recent years, however, the economics of annuities have improved. Modern studies across the globe and in Canada show that annuities now generally return 95 to 100 per cent of premiums paid, in present value terms. In fact, with the recent fall in long-term government bond yields, the value returned on many Canadian annuities has exceeded a 100 per cent return of premiums paid in many cases.

Another commonly cited reason for not annuitizing is that the retiree wants to leave a large lump sum to a survivor. This argument is not, however, especially compelling. Even when people have little or no intention of leaving assets behind for their heirs, there has been a baffling lack of interest in annuities. Economists have come to refer to this phenomenon as the "under-annuitization puzzle." The various proposed explanations for this puzzle all have an element of truth. They include:

- the desire to have money on hand for a rainy day;
- the fear of dying early and leaving all that money in the insurer's hands;
- the apparent low income in relation to the cost of the annuity;
- a reluctance to give up the chance to do better (within a RRIF) if stock markets do well; and
- the fact that other forms of retirement benefits, including government-sponsored pensions, already provide sufficient protection against longevity risk so the RRIF does not need to provide ironclad protection.

Annuitizing Later

If you are still not sold on annuities, you should know that they become even more attractive later in retirement. In other words, if you don't annuitize when you first retire, you still might want to do so later. Here's why.

Annuities start to look quite attractive by the time one has reached age 75. To understand why, let's look at the minimum pay-out at age 75 under a RRIF. If the RRIF held $100,000 in assets at age 75, the minimum amount that would have to be withdrawn that year is $7,850. As we have already seen, many retirees are upset about this because they feel their assets are depleting too quickly. But note that even in the current low-interest rate environment, an annuity at age 75 that is purchased with a single premium of $100,000 would produce annual income of nearly $10,000 or about $2,000 more than the RRIF. Moreover, the annuity removes any chance the assets will run out too soon because the payments are guaranteed for life.

Should You Annuitize?

We suggest that readers keep an open mind about annuities rather than automatically putting their RRSP monies into a RRIF at retirement. And if you still choose to go with the RRIF, you might want to consider purchasing an annuity later on, at around age 75 for the reasons given above.

18

When You Can No Longer Cope on Your Own

Jerry Seinfeld once famously observed that people are more afraid of public speaking than they are of death—which means they would prefer to be the guy in the casket than the one giving the eulogy! The prospect of requiring expensive care when we can no longer take care of ourselves is a little like that: in our retirement years, we seem to be more afraid of the cost of long-term care than we are of death. This fear is not even based on statistics: it is more visceral than that. Point out to anyone that spending takes a dive in Phase 2 of their retirement (which, as we saw, is a time of diminished mental or physical capacity) and the rejoinder invariably is, "Yeah, but what about long-term care?" This is the trump card in every argument about why we think we need to over-save and under-spend, even after retirement. It is also why we have trouble believing low retirement income targets.

If we take a harder look at our fears in the harsh light of day, we can finally put to rest our concerns about long-term care and get on with retirement. We need to understand better how many people will actually need long-term care at some point in their retirement years, and what the associated costs will be. For starters, care of the elderly in Canada is generally provided in one of three ways: home care, privately-run retirement homes, and government-run nursing homes.

Home Care

Home care (also sometimes called "home and community care") involves service providers coming into the home of the senior to perform services that are usually non-medical in nature, such as food preparation, housekeeping, laundry, assistance with bathing, monitoring medication, and supervision. Other services include physiotherapy and nursing care.

While home care often refers specifically to services provided by government agencies at no cost to the senior, the government's assistance has its limitations, and it is often necessary to supplement it with help from agencies and individuals in the private sector who will charge for their services. In addition, charitable institutions and volunteer organizations provide additional support at no charge or at subsidized rates. Of the many private sector providers that offer home care services on a for-profit basis, some private accreditation exists (e.g., personal support workers); still, the extent, quality, and cost of services from the private sector are highly variable, so buyers must shop around.

Usually, seniors who avail themselves of home care services have entered Phase 2 of their retirement. Here are two examples that involve a low to medium level of care:

- **Case 1:** An 85-year-old widow who has osteoarthritis and leg edema. The services she receives include meal delivery twice a day on weekdays, supervision while eating to prevent choking, and bathing twice a week plus assistance in putting on stockings each weekday morning. Some of these services are provided by government at no charge and some are provided by private sources.

- **Case 2:** A 72-year-old widower who lives in an apartment building in a small community. He has cataracts in both eyes and has been diagnosed with dementia. He tends to forget to take his medicines and does not eat properly. The services he receives include meals prepared in-home twice a day on weekends, bathing four times a week, supervision four times a week to help him get off the bus and back home without getting lost, laundry, and housecleaning. Once again, this involves a combination of government and private services, since government home care may only include bathing twice a week and would not include supervision to get on and off the bus.

Sometimes seniors in Phase 3 of retirement (when they are severely incapacitated by physical or mental issues) also receive home care, because they or their families insist on it rather than consignment to a nursing home. In these cases, a high level of care is required.

- **Case 3:** An 88-year-old woman who still lives with her 93-year-old husband in a condominium. She has had a recent stroke and is a diabetic. She can walk short distances but otherwise needs a wheelchair. Besides the types of services described above, a private nurse visits four times a week to monitor insulin use, check that medicines are being taken properly, and change the dressing on a heel ulcer.

In Case 1 (low-care scenario), the services would cost $500 to $1,000 a month, depending on how many hours the government is prepared to give versus how many need to be supplemented by private sources at a cost to the senior. In Case 2 (medium care), the services cost $1,000 to $1,500 a month. In Case 3 (high care), the cost is about $5,000 a month, but these cases are rare because most seniors in this situation would be in nursing homes. The cost in Case 3 can be less than $5,000 a month if the family of the senior engages a live-in caregiver.

A 2001 study found that about 14 per cent of seniors use home care services in a given year. Given that this includes younger seniors (those in the first phase of their retirement), the percentage of seniors in Phase 2 of retirement who require home care would be appreciably higher. For most of them, the low- or medium-care scenarios would apply.

Retirement Homes

Retirement homes would be appropriate for seniors in Phase 2 who do not need 24-hour availability of nursing care or specialized health services, and who cannot get the required level of attention at a reasonable cost from home care. Other reasons seniors go into retirement homes are because they are no longer sufficiently mobile to live on their own or because they feel too isolated in their homes. Most seniors are in their mid- to late-eighties by the time they enter a retirement home.

Besides accommodation, services that are typically offered include daily meals, laundry, linens, 24/7 availability of staff, outings, and regular fitness and social programs. Some retirement homes will also have an assisted-living floor, where residents can receive additional services (for which they also would pay more).

Retirement homes are usually provided by private sources and offer the full spectrum of levels of care. The cost ranges from $2,000 to $3,500 a month for fairly basic accommodation to up to $6,000 a month for a more luxurious setting. These figures include food, recreation, and utilities. One industry insider says it is very common to see seniors sell their home in order to pay for a potentially long stay in a retirement home.

Nursing Homes

Also referred to as "residential care" facilities or "long-term care" (LTC) facilities, nursing homes are recommended for those who need 24-hour nursing care or specialized services, which would normally mean people in Phase 3 of retirement. Only those with significant physical or mental disabilities are admitted into nursing homes, generally people who otherwise would require hospitalization, or at least constant medical attention. The residents tend to be older and the facility represents the final home for most of them. Nursing homes are government-run and provide the highest degree of care outside of hospitals. Besides 24-hour nursing care, regular doctor visits mean the patient does not have to leave the facility to see a doctor.

Nursing homes are the only long-term facility where the government pays for a majority of the costs of operation, including the cost of all medical care services. Most of the cost to the user therefore relates to accommodation, but there can be other user-paid services as well, such as food services outside of regular meals, manicures, hair styling, and a companion to accompany the senior for a regular walk. The cost for accommodation generally ranges from $1,000 to $2,000 a month depending on whether the room is a ward, semi-private, or private, with some further variation by province. Low-income seniors who cannot afford even the $1,000 monthly fee would turn over whatever pension they receive, and typically be left with a modest monthly allowance of $100 to $200. There is no fear anyone will be removed from a nursing home due to limited financial circumstances.

It is estimated that LTC residences will need to accommodate 518,000 residents by 2031, which will represent about 20 per cent of the entire Canadian population aged 80 and over. Most people in LTC residences, however, will be over 85, and about 35 per cent of the population over 85 will eventually find themselves in such a home. This should be a sustainable cost for the public purse given that the current LTC cost represents a small proportion of the country's current total healthcare budget.

Analysis

One can break down the financial concerns associated with long-term care by the different phases of retirement.

We'll start with the group that eventually reaches Phase 3 of retirement and will need to move to a nursing home. This does not apply to everyone, or even to a majority of people who reach an advanced age. Most people who live past 85 will stay in Phase 2 until the very end of their lives. The fact that one senior in three over 85 eventually finds their way to a nursing home means that the other two-thirds will continue to live in a retirement home, in their own homes, or with their families until death.

When viewed from the perspective of a 65-year-old who is considering his or her own long-term prospects, the odds of avoiding a nursing home are better again. A 65-year-old has about a 50/50 chance of surviving until 85 which means he or she has only a chance in six of eventually entering a nursing home. Even if they do, the cost will be covered by the government if they don't have the means. Anyone who has any significant RRSP savings will have the means for preferred accommodation in a nursing home, given that the cost is limited to about $2,000 a month, and the senior will have income in that range from OAS, CPP, and a small amount of income from a RRIF. In many cases, they wouldn't even have to sell their principal residence or take out a reverse mortgage to generate income. The bottom line is that entering a nursing home in Phase 3 of retirement marks a serious turn for the worse in one's health, which may be sad, but it isn't a financial problem.

Next, we will look at the retirees who remain in Phase 1 until death (or at least until a few months before death). We estimate that approximately 25 per cent of 65-year-olds will find themselves in this category. Their health costs will be minimal, given they are in reasonably good health by virtue of being in Phase 1, and they can probably look to a time in their eighties when they will have more money than they need because their spending will likely decline even if they don't officially enter into Phase 2. Clearly, the lucky ones who always remain in Phase 1 will not face any financial issues involving long-term care.

Finally, we consider the group that reaches Phase 2 of retirement. By applying mortality rates to people between ages 65 and 80, there is approximately a 25 per cent chance that a retiree will die before reaching Phase 2. Given that another 25 per cent or so stay in Phase 1 for their entire lives, it follows that about half the population will eventually encounter Phase 2. Most of them will be able to fend for themselves in Phase 2, apart perhaps from a low level of home care at low or modest cost in their more advanced years. Only a small percentage will eventually take up residence in a retirement home. In addition, some seniors will not go to a retirement home due to cost or preference and will instead live in their own home, or with family. We estimate there is a one-in-16 chance of eventually winding up in a retirement home.

We finally get to the crux of the issue. When you are 65 or so, your concern about whether you will have enough money to pay for long-term care really comes down to whether you are going to be the one person in 16 who will eventually find yourself in a retirement home or face similar costs through high-level home care. You have several ways to prepare yourself for that one-in-16 chance:

1. Do nothing. It may seem irresponsible but the odds are fairly low and, if worse comes to worst, you will be able to pay for a large part of your long-term care through your existing retirement income, which is fine since you will no longer be using it for any other purpose. If that is not enough, and if your

family will not pay for it, there is always the option of selling your home, which is already a common practice. No one said you need to leave a large estate to your children.

2. Buy LTC insurance. Insurance does exist through the various large insurance companies, banks, and independent agents. Benefits are paid monthly and currently range in cost from $20 to $300 a day. Examples of potential amounts of coverage available are 750 times the daily benefit amount, 2000 times the daily benefit amount, and unlimited. The policyholder can claim the benefit if he or she cannot perform two or more of six specified daily living activities. The premiums depend on age and gender. Depending on the policy, the premiums can be paid for up to 20 years or, if longer, the period up to 65; premiums can also be paid for life, although payments would be waived when an approved claim is made. To give a very rough idea, the monthly premiums are in the $200 range for a 55-year-old and in the $300 range for a 65-year-old.

3. Self-insure. This entails under-spending in retirement to save up enough just in case one does end up in a home. This is roughly what many Canadian retirees do, but without any attempt at quantifying how much they will actually need. Of course, the amounts they do set aside would represent a wasted spending opportunity and money to be passed along to the next generation if the need for it never arises or if they have overestimated the cost.

Given this analysis, the cost of long-term care when we can no longer fend for ourselves should be the least of our worries. The greater worry is that we may someday find ourselves in a situation in which our capacity to enjoy life has become limited and that perhaps cannot be helped. But should the response at this stage of our lives be to over-save, or to enjoy life while we can?

19

Tackling the Big Unknowns

Given the existing situation and emerging trends, we are gaining a clearer picture of how retirees in Canada will do over the next couple of decades. Adjustments will have to be made to our current thinking about retirement, but that's hardly a surprise. The universe will continue to unfold, sometimes in surprising and unexpected ways. The key is to anticipate as many changes as are reasonably predictable and to adjust our expectations and strategies accordingly.

First the Good News: You're in the Right Place

Canada has been accused of being smug about its comparatively sound financial situation vis-à-vis the rest of the world. While smugness is not our intent in these difficult times, it is comforting to know Canadians can face the future starting from a position of financial and political stability. We can only expect to maintain a strong social safety net, however, if we have the means to pay for it.

The financial crisis of 2008–2009 was seriously disturbing to many people around the world, but most decisively to citizens of the

European countries. The nations which literally banked on the Euro as a means of providing financial stability were shocked to discover that sharing a common currency strained the union to the breaking point when the various nations involved did not all treat their fiscal responsibilities with equal seriousness. The union worked as long as economic growth could paper over the cracks, but not when a real crisis surfaced. When countries such as Greece, Spain, Portugal, and Italy realized their deficits were beyond their control, they were forced to rely on the few more prudent European countries to bail them out. It was another version of the Aesop fable of the ant and the grasshopper, with the hardworking ant (Germany) not caring much to bail out the irresponsible grasshoppers.

It will take a few more years for the crisis to play itself out, but it has already delivered a few hard-learned lessons in financial responsibility. The truth is, financial crises have always been with us and always will be. We should expect that some other event of minor or major impact is sure to arise, and the volatility of our global economy is more likely to increase than decrease. Financial crashes come and go and various economies will grapple with new fiscal problems, but while individual countries and some regions pay a larger price than others, consistent growth will ultimately prevail. We see this continuing through 2025 and beyond, with Canada in a relatively stable place, building on a history of economic growth. Compared to other OECD and non-OECD countries, as reported by the World Bank, Canada has done very well on a GDP per capita basis over the last three decades.

On a global basis, the devastating impact of the 2008–2009 financial crisis manifested itself in the across-the-board negative growth in 2009. While the aftershocks of the crisis are still being felt, virtually all sectors recovered a major portion of their losses the following year. The sole exception was the EU, which recorded a drop for a second year, beginning in 2010, while continuing to grapple with its problematic debt and currency issues.

In contrast, Canada was the most successful nation at recovering from the trials of 2008–2009, recouping a significant part of the slippage in a single year. Many reasons have been offered for this success, the primary one being our staid but steady banking system, backed by the wealth generated by our considerable natural resources. Both factors, to one extent or another, can be expected to continue making their presence felt through the next two decades and beyond. This country indeed will remain among the best places to avoid the risk of catastrophic economic collapse. We will not be able to entirely avoid the impact of future crises elsewhere in the world, but we will be positioned at least as well as comparable countries in absorbing the blows and resuming growth.

As long as we're mining for good news, remember that CPP financing appears well-managed, dismissing any serious concerns about the program's abilities to meet future obligations.

The Clouds on the Horizon

By definition, GDP growth is powered primarily by private corporations whose fiscal philosophies are constricted by shareholder and ownership constraints. We can never assume that a corporation functions according to frugal principles, but any publicly traded company that builds excessive debt will find bankers and shareholders alike expressing their objections vigorously and directly.

Governments face more restrictions than they have in the past. Recent developments, including the ongoing dilemma in Europe associated with government overspending, has alerted other nations to the need for prudence. Canada is no exception. So what will the federal government do when the need to demonstrate thrift—i.e., a reduction in spending and an avoidance of increased taxation—clashes with growing expenditures to care for an aging population?

Among the questions to be faced:

- How will governments deal with the projected higher costs of health care in the next 20 years?

- Will the more affluent seniors be expected to absorb a greater share of health and pension costs in the process?

- Will we cope with our growing need for long-term care facilities?

- What further changes can we expect to Pillar 1 and Pillar 2 pension programs?

Without doubt, the darkest cloud hanging over us is the growing cost of health care. As we noted earlier, by far the majority of healthcare expenditures are consumed by seniors over 70 years of age. When private employers provided extended healthcare coverage to their retirees, this suggested a shift of weight and responsibility onto private sources. These extended benefits vanished long ago, and at least basic funding of health coverage has only one source: federal and provincial taxes.

Continually increasing health expenditures lead to higher per capita costs every year. The response of governments in the past was to meet the higher costs with higher taxes, but that source has a limit as well. Taxes *might* be raised further to address the funding dilemma, but *should* they be raised? A large and growing sector of Canadians say no, not without looking for other means. This is one of the big unknowns. Will out-of-pocket health expenditures borne by well-off retirees rise so much that they will need to gross up their retirement savings to pay for them?

Aside from paying for government-provided health care through taxes, where are Canadian households spending money to keep themselves and their families healthy? The most recent data, provided by

Statistics Canada from their CANSIM Database, indicates that the average annual expenditure on health care by household in 2009 was just over $2,000, a rise of about 77 per cent from the $1,133 spent just 12 years earlier. This level of expenditure will likely continue to rise faster than inflation. Of the total annual expenditure, more than 25 per cent was spent on prescribed and non-prescribed drugs, and another 25 per cent on private health insurance plans. The remaining half was directed toward dental care, eye care, and other peripheral services.

A Quick Look Back at the Private Sector's Response

As actuaries and consultants, we have been helping private companies deal with similar cost increases over the past 20 or so years. Employee benefits represented one of the fastest-growing areas of expense for companies from the mid-1980s onward, with increases of more than 5 per cent annually. It soon became evident that these increases were unsustainable, and CEOs began anxiously searching for ways to contain costs, beginning with the elimination of healthcare benefits for retirees, where this was possible. When unions resisted the idea, the companies were at least able to freeze existing benefits.

This slowed down the cost escalation but more was needed, so companies began eliminating services considered non-essential, then shifting at least some responsibility for payment from the company to individuals. This shift took the form of co-payments and deductibles, along with incentives for employees to think twice before deciding to use the health services in their plans.

It's apparent that shifting at least part of the costs to individuals is a strategy likely to be adopted by governments as well as private companies, to achieve the goal of stemming the rising tide of health-care expenses.

A Likely Model: U.S. Corporations and Their Benefits Programs

Canadian companies have it easier than their U.S. counterparts where employee health coverage is concerned. Nothing in the U.S. compares with Canada's universal healthcare coverage. The cost of providing private health insurance to qualified employees in the U.S. has become prohibitive enough for a growing number of companies to eliminate this benefit. Over the 12 years from 1999 to 2011, the number of U.S. firms offering health benefits for active employees fell from 66 to 60 per cent, while the number of workers covered by the benefits slid from 62 to 58 per cent.[1] That's not a precipitous drop, but it has been a slow and steady one. Efforts to extend coverage to all Americans are unlikely to result in corporations taking on more risk.

For retired employees, the change was dramatic. In 1998, fully two-thirds of large firms in the U.S. offered health benefits for their retired employees. By 2011, barely a quarter of them still provided coverage.[2]

U.S. firms and their healthcare providers have also instituted higher deductible amounts in a fairly short time period. The deductible levels vary widely by plan as well as by the service provider. For single coverage with employer health plans provided by HMOs (Health Maintenance Organizations—multi-discipline clinics that the employees must consult for coverage under their plan), annual deductibles, which averaged $352 in 2006, soared to $911 in 2011, an increase of almost 160 per cent in five years.[3]

The Challenge of Dealing with Downloading of Costs

What we've shown is that increasing healthcare costs are almost certainly going to lead federal and provincial governments to download some of the increases to individuals. It's how companies have managed cost increases, in both Canada and the U.S., and the government has already started down this path, with the introduction of income-testing in pensions, and means-testing in some areas of health care. The math of paying for the increases, as we've shown, just won't work without tax increases or downloading of costs. We think that means-testing or income-testing will be the easier political solution, and it will be sold on the premise that it will help fund health care for all. Those who have the means will be asked to pay, and in some cases, there will be fees, which will be intended to help you make the right decision on health care. But should this affect your financial planning? Will the costs be so significant that you need to save more, and that your NRIT needs to be higher? It all sounds bad, but what does it add up to?

We think the costs will be manageable, and that it will not affect financial planning in a major way. First, we go back to our history of health care in this country. There is widespread support for universal care and core healthcare services will always be there. The question will be the financing of new services, which are certain to require additional money. What you will, in fact, need in the future may not even exist right now. Twenty-five years ago, no one was worrying about how long it would take to get an MRI exam done—MRIs didn't exist, or, at least, they were not widely available. So, 25 years from now, there may be some new, better healthcare alternative and if you can afford to pay for it, there may be a cost. But there is really no way to plan for that. And if you're largely satisfied with your health care today—and most surveys say that's how most of us feel—then why plan for unknown improvements?

We go back to our phases of retirement to consider this conclusion a bit more carefully. In Phase 1, when you are largely healthy, we see the potential addition of some user fees on health care, or some means-testing for ancillary healthcare services. But to put it in context, the current total spending for health care for seniors between ages 65 and 74 is about $6,600 per person annually. Even if seniors in that age group are asked to absorb a 10 per cent increase, it's not likely to alter their financial plan in a major way. In Phases 2 and 3, when costs for government-provided health care really escalate (about $13,000 in 2009 dollars per person per year for seniors aged 75 to 84, and $23,500 per person per year for those aged 85 and older), it will be more difficult to pass costs along to the consumer. Even if means-testing were introduced in this later phase of life, which seems to be very unlikely given the perceived frailty and vulnerability of those who would be affected, it is too hard to quantify and unlikely to become a part of any reasonable financial plan. Seniors are lucky to live in a country where the political consensus is that the core healthcare needs for the elderly are supported through broadly based taxation.

As the source of universal health care in Canada, federal and provincial governments have begun reducing the scope of their benefits, a move that is bound to continue albeit in a gradual and incremental way, perhaps involving means-testing. Nevertheless, all this cost-shifting is unlikely to alter retirement planning in any fundamental way. Cost increases are likely to be focused on those most able to pay and will come primarily from new services.

The Long-Term Care Question

Much has been made about the high cost of the long-term care seniors require when they reach Phase 2 and especially Phase 3 of retirement. The very uncertainty surrounding the potential need for LTC in the case of a particular individual, the extent of the need, and the corresponding cost are what make LTC so hard to deal with. For those who worry about whether they will be able to make ends meet in retirement, LTC has been a large part of the problem. As we saw in the last chapter, however, the financing of LTC is manageable without our having to curtail spending severely in retirement to pay for it.

One More Time: Our Three-Pillar Retirement System Is Doing Well

We have noted on several occasions that the Canada/Quebec Pension Plan is well managed and well funded. On the other hand, OAS is financed out of cash flow, which explains why the retirement age is being raised to 67; this will reduce its impact on government budgets. The trend toward citizens taking more personal responsibility for financing their retirement, pushed by the virtual disappearance of traditional employer-funded and managed pensions and pulled by tax-incentive vehicles such as RRSPs, TFSAs, and PRPPs, will encourage this development. The costs of paying for a greater share of health and long-term care are almost certain to show up for those contemplating retirement in the next few decades. But with a strong core benefit, and a stronger retirement position coming from a later retirement, it looks to be manageable.

20

Ending on an Optimistic Note

The world is a changeable place, and aren't we glad it is? Or we should be. Change keeps us intrigued with our lives and the lives of others. It also admittedly forces us to deal with changes, many of them unexpected and not always welcome.

In our years of maturity, with careers and family established, we learn to accept change and prepare ourselves for it. The preparation benefits from insight, education, experience, and guidance, which is what this book has been all about, where retirement planning is concerned.

As we write this, the world is undergoing its latest round of changes. While no country and its citizens are immune to the effects of change, we Canadians have something of a spectator seat where various crises and developments, some unfolding and some waiting in the wings, are concerned. They include:

- The situation in Europe, where governments, having over-promised on benefits that they cannot now deliver, are attempting to persuade their citizens to pay the price. But after a few decades of expecting to retire at age 60 or earlier with fully indexed pensions, among other benefits, people are unwilling to relinquish the largesse, let alone settle the debt incurred already.

- The developing crisis in the U.S., which insists on spending about 10 per cent more each year than it recovers in taxes and finds itself with a political system so polarized and conflicted that it cannot effectively tackle the situation through legislation.

- The unresolved conflicts in the Middle East, plus the rising internal tension in China and Russia.

We have our own challenges to face in Canada, of course, but when compared with the rest of the world, they appear infinitely more solvable. Seen from the perspective of retirement planning, they are practically glowing. Summing up many of the points we made earlier, they include a number of solid considerations.

- Our core pension system is under control. The GIS/OAS system, supported by taxes, has actually been improved in terms of solvency, with the government gradually raising the retirement age to 67. The C/QPP plan, as analyzed by the CPP actuary, is in solid shape to deliver benefits for the next 75 years—and no, that's not a misprint.

- Poverty among the elderly may not be entirely eradicated, but it remains far below that of a generation or two ago, and at substantially lower levels than in other societies in the developed world. We can say with confidence that anyone who participated in the country's workforce during his or her career will be able to retire with dignity.

- A national consensus exists supporting the government's determination to ensure that future retirees will enjoy at least a minimal level of security and comfort, regardless of lower levels of economic growth and lower workforce participation rates.

Of Course, There Are Always Challenges

The biggest challenge faced by working Canadians may have more to do with expectations than with practicalities. For example, Canada enjoyed almost four decades of generally steady economic growth, planting in the minds of many citizens the concept of retiring at a relatively young age, enjoying comprehensive and universal health and long-term care—and still enjoying reasonable tax rates. These expectations will have to be tempered in the future. A resumption of a comparably long period of economic growth is not in sight, and extensive low-cost healthcare benefits are just not in the cards.

One reason for the change in health care, meaning we can expect either less care or more taxes (or perhaps even both), is the fact that the economic engine driving our tax base—fully-employed Canadians in their productive work years—is shrinking in inverse proportion to the number of senior citizens. It's the latter, of course, who consume most of the services paid for by the former.

As for funding retirement itself, some of us may recall the 1980s, when mutual funds and even bonds generated double-digit annual returns, helping to build up the pool of retirement assets at a rapid clip. For the next few years, that reality will sound more like the product of a mutual fund salesman's dream machine. Those returns simply will not be available in the foreseeable future. Low interest rates and correspondingly low real returns on investments will be with us for some time.

Prepare to Assume More Responsibility

Not every goal we may have for retirement will be achievable, at least not without all of us assuming a healthy dose of personal responsibility.

The most dramatic change may stem from the rising cost of health care. Governments will try to avoid raising taxes by shifting some of the burden onto individuals and perhaps redefining essential services. We are likely to continue to regard as essential the services provided to those most in need. Among wealthier Canadians, the number of core healthcare services available as a no-cost benefit may shrink, however, and consumers may be expected to pay for peripheral services. A similar extension of individual responsibility will apply to retirement planning—even more than is the case today. Respecting provision for both health care and retirement, governments will attempt to avoid widespread tax increases by pushing back increased costs to individual Canadians.

Before you permit these developments to worry you, look more closely at the situation.

- Much of the change regarding increased costs will be linked to affordability by both government and individuals. Healthcare services are unlikely to vanish, and costs are equally unlikely to reach unaffordable levels. If you are satisfied with health care now, you are likely to be satisfied with it in the future.

- The biggest question regarding pension income will concern how it is supplemented by individual retirees. The government-based portion is solid, and saving to generate higher pension amounts will be assisted by various tax breaks.

- More good news: you are probably going to live a longer and healthier life than your immediate ancestors. Before you ask, "But will I have enough money to live on for all of those years?" keep in mind that retirees are generally happy and most of the happiness they enjoy has little to do with their wealth.

One effective and profitable way of preparing yourself is to take charge of your finances. Your goals should include reducing your debts to zero by your expected retirement date, and building assets in an RRSP or TFSA through good management.

A large debt load can be the biggest headache related to the financial side of retirement. It will be like trying to hike with your friends while dragging an anchor chained to your leg. Debt prevents you from doing things, such as sleeping well at night. Aim to retire your debt on the day you yourself retire, if not sooner.

It is equally important to manage the investments that will finance your retirement. If your plan is being professionally managed, ensure that you understand the strategy, the tactics and the investments being used. Don't be afraid to ask questions about any investment you do not understand, and invest at least a few minutes each day to read the business section of your newspaper or watch investment-oriented television shows dealing with the financial situation and its direction.

Among the most important concepts to grasp are the differing roles of equities and fixed-income investments in your portfolio. While both can build their value over time, equities provide the better long-term opportunity, riding over market fluctuations, while fixed-term instruments, such as bonds, GICs, and treasury bills, ensure stability. The closer you approach your planned retirement, the more stability your portfolio needs.

Finally, keeping an eye on the performance of your investments is always a good policy. Changing them often is not. Try to make your decisions carefully, supported by professional advice, and avoid frequent buying and selling.

The False Glory of Retiring Early

Perhaps no expectation about retirement has changed, and continues to change, more than the concept of when to retire. The "Freedom 55" theme featured by a life insurance company in the early 1990s may have been effective as a marketing ploy, but it was less successful in real life. Instead of focusing on shifting from employment to retirement virtually overnight, attention should be paid to the bigger question, the one that asks, "What will I do when and after I retire?" In other words, *start defining your expectations.*

Many stories exist about Canadians seizing the opportunity to walk away from their work careers and, soon after the initial euphoria wears off ("I'm free!"), finding that they have shed more than their work—they also have lost their identity and purpose. We all need to recognize what we will face in retirement and plan accordingly, based on some realizations discussed earlier. They include:

- You likely will not need as much money in your retirement years as many experts have suggested. Yes, you will require more health care and other attention, especially as your age advances, but their costs will not threaten your financial security. Given some basic planning (a paid-off mortgage, zero major debts, no dependants at home) you should be able to live fairly comfortably with retirement income representing 50 per cent of your pre-retirement earnings.

- This is reassuring, because returns on the investments in your retirement portfolio are likely to be lower than you may have hoped just a few years ago.

- Your value as a productive employee will remain high and may even soar, because many companies won't have enough experienced workers to get the work done. This may lead to a gradual reduction of your weekly work hours and an extension of your working career before full retirement, an effective way of handling the lower returns on your retirement fund investments.

- In fact, more of your friends and co-workers will also choose to retire later, giving you another incentive to remain on the job for a few more years. After all, why retire if your friends are at work all day?

- Employers won't fill the gap in health care or pensions, but may be more likely to reward you in cash than in benefits.

Take Charge of Your Life!

Obviously these developments involve some decision-making on your part. This shouldn't be frightening or disturbing. You are reaching a time in your life when you should feel confident, not only about deciding what is best for you, but in empowering yourself to select the best way to reach that goal. For example, retiring later than planned should be seen as a plus, because it helps you ease into a new chapter in your life, sampling and selecting the things that appeal to you, and avoiding those you can do without. The best route is working part-time to maintain work contacts and confirm that you remain valuable and productive.

This may involve entering into negotiations with your employer, which puts some decision-making power in your hands. If that's the case, remember to be flexible with your expectations. Consider accepting a more modest pay package than you may have expected, if the arrangement permits you to enjoy more leisure time, and perhaps match your working hours to interests you have beyond your work.

Finally, much of the enjoyment we gather from life is a matter of perspective. The person who refuses even the smallest amount of adventure because he or she is afraid of dying never truly lives. No, we don't need to go sky-diving or climb Mount Everest. We only need to live now and enjoy the moment rather than worrying unduly about the future.

People who focus their attention too much on planning for their retirement risk missing too much of their life *before* retirement, and that's a tragedy. It's fine to plan and be prudent, and obviously it's wise to take a serious look at planning for your retirement years. But having reviewed your plans and made your prudent decisions, be sure to leave enough time and money for the life you are living *today*. Instead of salting away every available loonie into your retirement fund, invest some in life. Take your spouse on a weekend trip to a destination you've never visited before. Save and splurge on a pair of shoes or skis you've always wanted. Or just take your grandkids (or yourself) out to fly a kite on a lovely summer's day.

Life may be precious, but not so precious that you need to lock it away in a vault. Take it into the world and enjoy it, every day you can.

Appendix A: Pillar 1 and Pillar 2 Benefits

This appendix summarizes the benefits under Pillars 1 and 2, including changes that are currently being phased in. Below are benefits as of mid-2012.

Table A.1: Benefits from CPP, OAS, and GIS Payable by Age

June–July 2012 Maximum Pension Benefits by Age	Age 60 (Old Rates)	Age 60 (Future Rates)	Age 65	Age 70 (Old Rates)	Age 70 (Future Rates)
CPP	$690.67	$631.47	$986.67	$1,282.67	$1,401.07
OAS	Not Eligible	Not Eligible	$540.12	$540.12	$734.56
GIS					
Single person	Not Eligible	Not Eligible	$732.36	$732.36	$732.36
Spouse of person receiving OAS pension	Not Eligible	Not Eligible	$485.61	$485.61	$485.61
Spouse of person not receiving OAS pension	Not Eligible	Not Eligible	$732.36	$732.36	$732.36

Table A.2: Benefits from CPP, OAS, and GIS Payable by Income Level

June–July 2012 Maximum Pension Benefits by Family Income Level	$15,000/ yr	$30,000/ yr	$60,000/ yr	$90,000/ yr	$120,000/ yr
CPP	$986.67	$986.67	$986.67	$986.67	$986.67
OAS	$540.12	$540.12	$540.12	$284.65	$0
GIS					
Single person	$253.19	$0	$0	$0	$0
Spouse of person receiving OAS pension	$318.94	$0	$0	$0	$0
Spouse of person not receiving OAS pension	$617.78	$253.19	$0	$0	$0

Table A.3: CPP, OAS, and GIS Benefits and Income Cut-offs, 2012

	Average Benefit Jan. 2012	Maximum Benefit	Maximum Annual Income Cut-off* (June 2012)	Maximum Annual Income Cut-off for Top-ups (June 2012)
CPP (at age 65)	$527.96	$986.67 (2012)	NA	NA
OAS	$510.21	$540.12 (July 2012)	NA	NA
GIS				
Single person	$492.26	$732.36 (July 2012)	$16,368	$4,448
Spouse of person receiving OAS pension	$309.28	$485.61 (July 2012)	$21,648	$7,456
Spouse of person not receiving OAS pension	$468.55	$732.36 (July 2012)	$39,264	$8,896

*The maximum annual income cut-off refers to the highest annual income before no longer being eligible for any amount of the GIS benefit. It does not include OAS income or the first $3,500 of employment income.

Eligibility Age Raised for OAS and GIS

The 2012 federal budget proposed increasing the age of eligibility for Old Age Security (OAS) and Guaranteed Income Supplement (GIS) benefits gradually from age 65 to 67 starting in April 2023. The change will be fully implemented by January 2029. This proposed change to OAS/GIS eligibility will not affect anyone 54 years of age or older as of March 31, 2012, which means individuals who were born on March 31, 1958, or earlier will not be affected. Those who were born on or after February 1, 1962, will have an age of eligibility of 67. Those who were born between April 1, 1958, and January 31, 1962, will have an age of eligibility between 65 and 67, in accordance with Table A.4.

Table A.4: OAS/GIS Age of Eligibility by Date of Birth

MONTH OF BIRTH	1958	1959	1960	1961	1962
	OAS/GIS ELIGIBILITY AGE				
January	65	65 + 5 months	65 + 11 months	66 + 5 months	66 + 11 months
February–March	65	65 + 6 months	66	66 + 6 months	67
April–May	65 + 1 month	65 + 7 months	66 + 1 month	66 + 7 months	67
June–July	65 + 2 months	65 + 8 months	66 + 2 months	66 + 8 months	67
August–September	65 + 3 months	65 + 9 months	66 + 3 months	66 + 9 months	67
October–November	65 + 4 months	65 + 10 months	66 + 4 months	66 + 10 months	67
December	65 + 5 months	65 + 11 months	66 + 5 months	66 + 11 months	67

In line with the increase in age of OAS/GIS eligibility, the ages at which the Allowance and the Allowance for the Survivor are provided will also gradually increase from 60–64 today to 62–66 starting in April 2023. This change will not affect anyone 49 years of age or older as of March 31, 2012. Certain federal programs, including those for veterans and aboriginals that provide income support benefits until age 65, will be aligned with changes to the OAS program, so that these individuals do not face a gap in income between 65 and 67.

Option to Defer OAS

Starting on July 1, 2013, the federal budget will allow for the voluntary deferral of the OAS pension for up to five years. Those who choose to defer will receive a higher, actuarially adjusted, annual pension. The adjustment would be a 0.6 per cent increase in OAS pension for each month that commencement is deferred. This is less generous than the 0.7 per cent increase that applies under the Canada/Quebec Pension Plans between 65 and 70. It does give Canadians added flexibility in planning for their retirement and does so on a cost-neutral basis. GIS benefits will not be eligible for actuarial adjustment.

Appendix B: Income by Source

This table shows the breakdown of income by source for Canadians 55 and over.

Table B.1: Income by Source for Canadians 55 and Over

Year	Median Income (Dollars)	From Employment	From Investment	From Gov.	From Private Pension	From RRSP	From Other
			Ages 55 to 64				
2000	$23,500	64.8%	7.3%	9.2%	13.4%	0.0%	5.3%
2001	$24,800	65.7%	7.1%	8.9%	13.3%	0.0%	5.1%
2002	$25,800	66.6%	6.0%	8.9%	13.2%	0.0%	5.2%
2003	$26,800	67.6%	5.8%	8.6%	13.0%	0.0%	4.9%
2004	$28,000	68.3%	5.8%	8.3%	12.7%	0.0%	4.9%
2005	$29,300	68.8%	5.9%	8.0%	12.3%	0.0%	5.0%
2006	$30,700	68.8%	6.5%	7.7%	11.8%	0.0%	5.2%
2007	$32,270	69.2%	6.9%	7.4%	11.4%	0.0%	5.1%
2008	$33,400	69.1%	7.2%	7.5%	11.2%	0.0%	5.0%
2009	$33,520	68.7%	6.9%	8.1%	11.4%	0.0%	4.9%

Year	Median Income (Dollars)	From Employment	From Investment	From Gov.	From Private Pension	From RRSP	From Other
			Age 65 and over				
2000	$17,500	9.5%	14.7%	43.5%	26.6%	2.5%	3.3%
2001	$18,100	9.8%	14.8%	42.9%	26.9%	2.3%	3.2%
2002	$18,500	10.3%	12.6%	43.7%	28.0%	2.3%	3.2%
2003	$18,800	10.6%	11.9%	43.8%	28.3%	2.2%	3.2%
2004	$19,400	11.0%	11.4%	43.3%	28.8%	2.1%	3.4%
2005	$20,100	11.7%	11.0%	42.5%	28.9%	2.1%	3.7%
2006	$21,000	12.2%	11.8%	41.5%	28.7%	1.9%	3.9%
2007	$22,110	12.9%	12.5%	40.3%	28.7%	1.8%	3.8%
2008	$22,820	13.3%	12.7%	40.0%	28.4%	1.7%	3.8%
2009	$23,110	13.4%	12.3%	41.1%	28.2%	1.8%	3.3%

Source: Statistics Canada. CANSIM Database, Table 202–0404.

Appendix C: NRIT Charts

The neutral retirement income targets (NRITs) shown below have been prepared under various scenarios and for a range of income levels. They include RRSP savings rates needed to reach those targets and the account balance you should be aiming for within your RRSP by retirement age.

Common Assumptions

1. The household includes a couple, both of whom are wage-earners.

2. The focus is on households in the upper three income quintiles: the bottom two quintiles earn less than the average national wage; most can expect additional pension on a means-tested basis.

3. The couple own a home and have paid off the mortgage by retirement.

4. The mortgage payments represented 25 per cent of their gross household income for 25 years.

5. Contributions are made to an RRSP at a constant percentage of pay starting at age 30.

6. The RRSP earns a return after fees of 5.75 per cent per annum.

7. The RRSP is transferred to a RRIF at retirement and earns the same 5.75 per cent annually.

8. The income that is withdrawn from the RRIF increases annually with inflation, assumed to be 2.25 per cent per annum.

9. The couple receive a CPP pension that is 10 per cent less than the maximum payable at their earnings level. The 10 per cent reduction reflects more years of low earnings than the 17 per cent dropout provision allowed by CPP.

10. Any expenditures not incurred every year in the pre-retirement period are assumed to be spread evenly over 35 years up until age 65.

Scenario 1

1. The couple have two children.

2. Expenditures for each child equal 10 per cent of gross income for 21 years.

3. By the time they retire at 65, the couple no longer need to support their children.

Figure C.1 shows how the neutral retirement income targets vary by income level.

Figure C.1: NRIT—Scenario 1

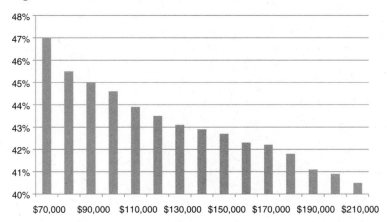

Generally, the NRIT ranges between 40 and 50 per cent of final earnings and falls by about 1 per cent for each $20,000 increase in household income.

The corresponding savings rates and RRSP balance at retirement charts are shown in Chapter 12.

Scenario 2

The next scenario assumes the couple has no children, which means they will have higher disposable income available for consumption during their working years and this leads to a higher NRIT so they can continue that higher level of consumption after retirement.

Figure C.2 shows the NRIT is higher across the board by about 10 to 12 per cent of pay versus Scenario 1. Having children makes a big difference. The NRIT as a percentage is also remarkably flat, varying by less than 4 per cent of final pay between the low and high ends of the income range.

Figure C.2: NRIT—Scenario 2

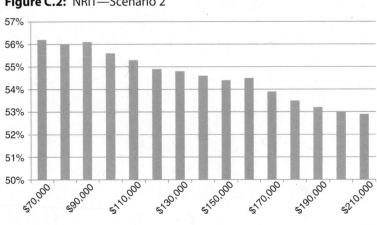

Figure C.3 shows the savings rates needed to reach the NRIT.

Figure C.3: Savings Rate—Scenario 2

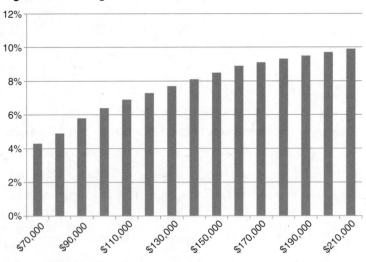

Compared to Scenario 1, the required savings rate is higher by about 3 per cent of pay but should be manageable given this couple has no child-related expenses. Childless couples grow accustomed to higher consumption during their working years and will expect it continue after retirement.

Figure C.4 shows the RRSP balance that corresponds to the savings rates in Figure C.3.

Figure C.4: RRSP Balance at 65—Scenario 2

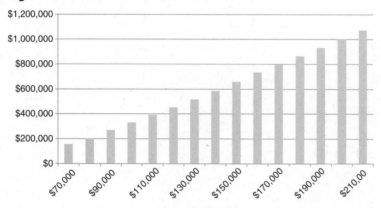

Appendix D: A Guide to Retirement Programs in Canada

This document was prepared by Morneau Shepell actuaries to provide an overview of employer-sponsored retirement programs in Canada. It focuses on group plans rather than individual plans and on plans that are *registered*—in other words, those that are tax-assisted and government-regulated.

Types of Retirement Programs

Retirement programs can be characterized by the type of benefits they provide. The main types are:

- **Defined benefit (DB) plans:** In a DB plan, the employer assumes most or all of the financial risk. The employer contributions are dependent on how well the pension fund investments perform, in addition to a variety of factors such as turnover, retirement patterns, and mortality.

- **Capital accumulation plans (CAPs):** In a CAP, the employee assumes the financial risk and the employer contributions are usually a stable percentage of pay.

Defined Benefit Plans

A DB plan provides a pension benefit that is defined in terms of the employee's length of service and/or earnings. If an employer were to adopt a DB plan today, it would probably be one of the three types described below.

1. *Flat dollar* plans provide a fixed amount of pension for each year of credited service (e.g., $50 of monthly pension for each year of credited service). This has been the plan of choice for unionized employees who are paid hourly wages.

2. *Final Average Earnings (FAE)* plans provide a pension based on a percentage of the employee's average earnings for each year of credited service. Average earnings can be calculated in a number of ways—for example, the best three consecutive years of earnings in the last 10 years prior to retirement, or the best five years of earnings, whether consecutive or not.

3. *Indexed Career Average Earnings* (CAE) plans provide members with a pension based on their earnings in each year they are a member of the plan. In the modern version of a CAE plan, the pension earned for a given year is indexed (i.e., increased) to reflect the change in average national wages for each year from the year the pension is earned until retirement. This is essentially how the Canada Pension Plan works.

Capital Accumulation Plans

A CAP defines the employer (and employee) contribution rate, not the benefit. The employer contribution rate may be a fixed percentage of an employee's salary, or a percentage of the contributions made by the employee. As a result, the employer cost from one year to the next will be much less volatile than with a DB plan.

In a CAP, a separate account is maintained for each employee. Contributions are credited with investment earnings—usually on a daily basis. Most CAPs allow employees to choose from a number of investment options. When an employee retires from a CAP, he or she can choose to purchase an annuity or transfer the account balance to a life income fund (*LIF*).

If an employee chooses to purchase an annuity from an insurance company, the amount of retirement income will depend on:

- the account balance;
- the prevailing interest rates;
- current age;
- type of annuity purchased.

If an employee chooses to transfer the account balance to an LIF, the amount of retirement income will depend on:

- the account balance; and
- investment returns generated after the employee retires.

The four primary types of CAPs are described below.

1. *Defined Contribution (DC)* plans are registered pension plans (*RPPs*) and as such, are subject to regulation by a combination of Canada Revenue Agency (CRA) and either a provincial pension regulator* or the Office of the Superintendent of Financial Institutions (OSFI). Most, but not all, DC plans require employees to make contributions.

2. *Group Registered Retirement Savings Plans (RRSP)* are a collection of individual RRSPs. In many ways, group RRSPs are

---

*There is no provincial regulator in PEI.

very similar to DC plans; however, there are some significant differences:

- Group RRSPs are not as heavily regulated.

- Employer contributions to group RRSPs must be made "indirectly." To be considered an indirect contribution, *the employer must add the desired contribution amount to* an employee's gross pay. The amount can then be deducted from the employee's payroll as an RRSP contribution. This process will increase the employer's other payroll-related costs such as life insurance, Canada Pension Plan (CPP) contributions, and Employment Insurance (EI).

3. *Deferred Profit Sharing Plans (DPSP)* are plans by which the employer makes contributions out of current or retained profits. Employees are not allowed to make contributions. Often, a group RRSP is combined with a DPSP so that employees can make contributions to the RRSP and the employer can make its matching contribution through the DPSP.

4. *Group Tax-Free Savings Accounts (TFSA)* are a new type of plan that became available in 2009. They are similar to RRSPs in the following ways:

- Employer contributions to a Group TFSA must be made indirectly.

- Investment earnings are tax-sheltered.

Group TFSAs differ from RRSPs in two major ways—contributions to a TFSA must be made with money that has already been taxed and withdrawals made from a TFSA are not subject to tax. Individuals can contribute up to $5,000 to a TFSA in a calendar year. This type of account is a good supplemental plan for high earners, or for younger employees who are more interested in short-term savings than a future retirement income.

Hybrid Plans

Some plans have both DB and CAP features, and are often called hybrid plans. We believe that the range of permissible hybrid plans may be expanded considerably in the near future. For instance, target benefit plans may be introduced. They look like DB plans but the employer contribution is fixed, as in a DC plan. See Figure D.1 for an overview of these plans.

Figure D.1: Characteristics of the Various Plan Types

	DB PLANS	DC PLANS	GROUP RRSPs	DPSPs	GROUP TFSAs
REGULATORY ISSUES					
Compliance with Pension Standards Legislation	Required	Required	Not required	Not required	Not required
Level of professional expertise required to maintain registration	High	Medium	Low	Low	Low
Ability to terminate plan or change to another plan type	Difficult, time-consuming	Less difficult	Not difficult	Not difficult	Not difficult
SPECIAL CONDITIONS					
Ability to enhance past service benefits	Yes	No	No	No	No
Protection of entitlements from creditors (excluding on marriage breakdown)	Yes	Yes	Yes, under certain conditions	No	No
EMPLOYEE'S RIGHT TO TRANSFER MONEY OUT					
While in active service	Not permitted Exception: AVC's	Same as DB plans	May be restricted by the employer	Same as group RRSPs	Same as group RRSPs

(Continued)

Figure D.1: *Continued*

	DB PLANS	DC PLANS	GROUP RRSPs	DPSPs	GROUP TFSAs
Upon death	Beneficiary must be spouse unless right is waived	Same as DB plans	No restrictions on beneficiary	Same as group RRSPs	Same as group RRSPs
Upon retirement or termination of employment before retirement	Monthly pension plan may permit lump sum transfer	Purchase annuity from an insurance company or lump sum transfer	Same as DC plans	Same as group RRSPs	Cash withdrawal or transfer to another TFSA
Longest *vesting* period an employer may impose	Two years except immediate vesting in Quebec	Two years except immediate vesting in Quebec	Immediate vesting	Two years of membership	Immediate vesting
Choice of vehicles for lump sum transfer	*LIRA*, LIF, other RPP, life annuity	Same as DB plans	RRSP, *RRIF*, RPP, annuity or cash	RPP, RRSP, DPSP, annuity or cash	TFSA or cash withdrawal
Locking-in (i.e., no access to money before retirement)	Applies	Applies	Does not apply	Does not apply	Does not apply
CONDITIONS ON EMPLOYER (ER) CONTRIBUTIONS					
Maximum tax-deductible contributions	Based on actuary's recommendation	The combined ER/EE DC pension limit*	Combined ER/EE limit of 18% of prior year earned income[†]	18% of *pensionable earnings* up to 50% of the DC pension limit	Combined EE/ER contributions may not exceed $5,000 per calendar year

(Continued)

Figure D.1: *Continued*

	DB PLANS	DC PLANS	GROUP RRSPs	DPSPs	GROUP TFSAs
Ability to make contributions in respect of past service	Yes, with some limitations	No	Yes, if employee has unused RRSP contribution room	No	Yes, if employee has unused TFSA room from prior years
CONDITIONS ON EMPLOYEE (EE) CONTRIBUTIONS					
Ability to make contributions that are not tax-deductible	None for current service, permitted for past service	No	Up to $2,000 deductible in future years	No	Yes, all contributions are made by the employee and are not deductible
Maximum tax-deductible contributions	Lesser of 70% of PA plus $1,000, or 9% of earnings up to a dollar limit‡	The combined ER/EE money purchase limit	See above	Employee contributions not allowed	N/A
Ability to make contributions in respect of past service	As required by plan; can be deducted up to $3,500/year ($5,500 in Quebec)	No	Yes, if employee has unused RRSP contribution room	No	Yes, if employee has unused TFSA room from prior years
Whether a PAR is generated on termination of employment	Yes, if entitlement is paid in a lump sum	Yes, to the extent entitlement not vested	No PAR	Yes, to the extent entitlement not vested	No PAR

(Continued)

Figure D.1: *Continued*

	DB PLANS	DC PLANS	GROUP RRSPs	DPSPs	GROUP TFSAs
Ability to carry forward unused contribution room	N/A	Not usually	Not usually	Yes	Yes
What payouts are taxable?	Pension payments; unlocked transfer values paid in cash	Unlocked transfer values paid in cash	Any amounts taken as cash payouts	Any amounts taken as cash payouts	None
What payouts are not taxable?	Transfers to a LIRA or LIF	Same as DB plans	Transfers to an RRSP or RRIF	Transfers to an RRSP or RRIF	All

*The DC pension limit for a given year is 18% of pensionable earnings up to a limit. The limit is $23,820 in 2012 and is indexed thereafter in line with annual increases in average wages for Canada.

†The RRSP limits shown assume no participation in another registered retirement program. The limits would be reduced by the PA for the prior year under RPPs and DPSPs. The same dollar caps would apply as for DC plans but with a one-year lag (e.g., $23,820 in 2013).

‡The dollar limit for employee contributions to DB plans is $17,254 in 2012, and is indexed thereafter.

Glossary

Active Management

Refers to the management of an investment portfolio where the manager attempts to outperform the market or some benchmark index rather than mirror the market. The opposite is passive management.

Annuity

A typical annuity is a series of fixed payments at regular intervals (usually monthly) lasting for life but often with benefits to be payable to a beneficiary or the estate after death. The term "annuity" is often used interchangeably with the term "life annuity," which refers to an immediate annuity that lasts for the entire lifetime of the person receiving payments from the annuity.

Asset Bubble (e.g., Housing Bubble, Stock Market Bubble)

A rapid rise in the price of an asset class beyond its fundamental value based on standard valuation metrics. Asset bubbles can last for many years before prices return, usually suddenly, to their fundamental value or below.

Asset Mix

The composition of a portfolio broken down by the major investment categories (e.g., 70 per cent equities/30 per cent fixed income).

AVC

Additional Voluntary Contributions—contributions that an employee may be permitted to make to a pension plan. They do not generate matching employer contributions.

Basis Points (bps)

Used to measure investment fees. One hundred basis points equals one per cent.

Bear Market

A falling market characterized by negative sentiment pertaining to a class of assets such as the stock market or fixed-income market. The opposite of a bull market.

Bond Yield

Refers to the effective interest rate, compounded annually, that is earned on a bond over its life.

Bull Market

A rising market characterized by positive sentiment pertaining to a class of assets such as the stock market or fixed-income market.

CAP

Capital Accumulation Plan—an investment or savings plan where the individual makes contributions which accumulate with interest. Examples of a CAP would be an RRSP or a TFSA.

CPI

Consumer Price Index—an indicator of inflation that measures change in the cost of a fixed basket of products and services including housing, electricity, food, and transportation.

CPP

Canada Pension Plan—an earnings-based government pension program. It constitutes the second pillar of Canada's three-pillar pension system. It was established in 1966 and is funded by equal employee and employer contributions of 4.95 per cent each of covered pay. The maximum pension at age 65 is 25 per cent of covered earnings and is indexed to inflation. Pension benefits can begin anytime between age 60 and 70. Contributions and pensions are based on employment earnings up to a level that is approximately equal to the average national wage.

CRA

Canada Revenue Agency—the governmental body that administers the Income Tax Act.

Defined Benefit Pension Plan

One of the two major types of pension plans where the benefit is defined in terms of an employee's earnings and/or length of service but not on the return of the underlying assets.

Defined Contribution Pension Plan

The other type of pension plan where the employer's contribution is defined in terms of the employee's pay or length of service and the pension is the amount that the accumulated contributions with interest can buy.

DPSP

Deferred Profit Sharing Plan—a tax-assisted arrangement to which employers can make tax-deductible contributions out of profits; employees cannot contribute to a DPSP.

Equities

Stocks or shares in publicly traded corporations.

FAE Plan

Final average earnings plan—a defined benefit plan where the pension is based on the employee's best average earnings in the few years just before retirement.

Fixed Income

Bonds and other debt instruments where a promised fixed rate of return is earned over time.

Flat Dollar Plan

A defined benefit plan where the pension is based on a fixed dollar amount multiplied by the number of years of credited service.

GICs

Guaranteed Investment Certificates—a Canadian investment vehicle that works like a government bond but usually cannot be resold. Individuals deposit a principal with the provider (usually a commercial bank), which is locked-in for some investment period (one, three, five, etc. years). The provider returns the principal plus accrued interest at the end of the term for the GIC. GICs are generally completely riskless and hence have returns that are on par with government bonds of similar duration.

GIS

Guaranteed Income Supplement—a supplementary benefit on top of OAS benefits, to low-income seniors in Canada who are receiving OAS benefits. GIS is a needs-based government retirement benefit to ensure that seniors, who are not receiving sufficient income from CPP and OAS, are provided with enough additional income to bring them up to a basic standard of living. It is subject to an income test and the amount of the supplement is reduced by earned income. The basic benefit amount can be grossed up to make up for the loss of OAS benefits due to not meeting the full residency requirement for OAS. It was introduced alongside the CPP in 1967. In 2011 a new additional top-up benefit was introduced for GIS recipients who have very low income.

Income Quintile (Households)

A 20 per cent tranche of households sorted by income level. For example, the first income quintile is the lowest 20 per cent of households by income level.

Index Fund

An open-ended investment fund that seeks to track the exact performance of a given index of stocks or other assets. It often uses derivatives as well as the purchase of a basket of stocks to achieve its aims. It is the most common form of a passively managed fund.

Investment Horizon

The period over which one should monitor or measure one's investment results.

LIF

Life Income Fund—a vehicle into which locked-in pension benefits can be transferred. It is a specific type of RRIF that exists for LIRAs and locked-in RSPs. There are additional limits on the maximum amount that can be withdrawn per year. In some provinces there is a mandated age at which a LIF must be converted to a life annuity.

LIRA

Locked-in Retirement Account—a vehicle into which locked-in pension benefits can be transferred. It's a specific type of RRSP, and virtually identical to locked-in RSPs. New contributions are not allowed and an account can only be established with transfers from terminated registered pension plan accounts. The funds are locked in and must be transferred to a life annuity, LIF, or LRIF to produce income. The specific limits on what age the transfers can occur and specific alternatives on transfer destinations differ from province to province.

Locking In

A term indicating that the employee must use it to secure lifetime retirement income rather than withdrawing it as a lump sum cash payment. Group RRSPs and DPSPs are not subject to minimum locking-in provisions.

Longevity Risk

The risk of running out of money before one dies.

LRIF

Locked-in Retirement Income Fund—a specific type of RRIF that exists for LIRAs and locked-in RSPs and is meant to be an alternative to LIFs. It differs from LIFs in that the maximum annual withdrawal amount is based on investment earnings in the previous year and not on age. Also any unused amounts to the maximum withdrawal are carried forward to future years.

Money Market Fund

An open-ended mutual fund that invests in short-term debt securities such as short-term government bonds/treasury bills and short-term commercial paper. In theory, they are intended to be virtually risk-free and not give rise to capital gains or losses. They typically offer a slightly higher yield than savings accounts but a lower yield than GICs since the funds invested are not locked-in as they are with GICs.

Nominal Returns

Investment returns that have not been adjusted for inflation.

OAS

Old Age Security—introduced in 1952 to replace a means-tested old age pension. It is a universal government retirement pension provided to all Canadian residents aged 65 and over who meet a residency requirement. The minimum residency requirement is 10 years for those currently living in Canada and 20 years for those currently living outside Canada. 1/40th of the full pension is paid for each year of residency—to a maximum of 40 years—once the minimum requirement is met. The current full pension is $540.12 per month (July 2012). Since 1989 there is a clawback on the pension. 15 per cent of earned family income above a prescribed limit ($69,562 in 2012) is taxed back until the pension is completely eliminated. Recent changes from the 2012 budget are: eligibility age is raised from 65 to 67 in stages by 2029; and pension can now be deferred up to age 70 with the pension amount increased by 0.6 per cent for each month commencement is deferred beyond 65.

OSFI

Office of the Superintendent of Financial Institutions—the body responsible for administering the Pension Benefits Standards Act (1985), which applies to employees in federally regulated industries.

PA

Pension Adjustment—as set out in the Income Tax Act, a PA is assigned to the benefits earned under registered pension plans in order to determine an individual's ability to contribute to an RRSP.

PAR

Pension Adjustment Reversal—RRSP contribution room that is restored to an individual who is enrolled in a registered pension plan or DPSP and who terminates employment, receiving a lump sum settlement rather than a pension.

Passive Management

Refers to the style of managing an investment portfolio that simply tries to replicate the performance of the market or of a given index. The opposite is active management.

Pensionable Earnings

An employee's earnings for pension purposes, as is defined in applicable pension documents. This may be different from the employee's earned income as defined for tax purposes.

QPP

Quebec Pension Plan—the sister pension program to the CPP, established with the CPP. It is for Quebec residents only. It was virtually identical to the CPP (same contribution rates and benefits) except for some differences in the ancillary benefits (survivor and disability benefits). Recently, the required contribution level was increased in phases and is now higher than under the CPP.

Real Returns

Investment returns net of inflation.

Registered

When applied to a pension plan, indicates that the plan has met certain regulatory requirements.

RPP

Registered Pension Plan—a tax-assisted pension plan that must be registered.

RRIF

Registered Retirement Income Fund—a tax-sheltered vehicle registered under the Income Tax Act, from which a retiree must make minimum withdrawals annually. They have the same tax treatment as RRSPs but there is an obligatory minimum annual withdrawal amount based on prescribed annuity factors and the remaining fund balance. No additional contributions can be made to RRIFs. It is designed as a vehicle to deplete accumulated RRSP savings to support retirement spending over one's remaining life.

RRSP

Registered Retirement Savings Plan—a vehicle to which tax-deductible contributions can be made. Contributions to RRSPs are tax deductible and limited to the smallest of 18 per cent of previous year's earned income and $22,970 (2012 limit; limit is indexed to national average wage). Unused contributions can be carried forward for up to 10 years. Withdrawals are taxed as regular income in the year they are taken. All RRSP funds must be converted to RRIF funds by no later than the seventy-first birthday. Funds from other tax deferred retirement savings vehicles such as registered pension plans that share the RRSP contribution limit can be transferred to an RRSP without tax implications.

S&P 500 Index

The Standard & Poor 500 Index is a floating market-value weighted index of 500 common stocks belonging to 500 publicly traded large-cap companies that are actively traded on either the NYSE or the NASDAQ. The index is considered to be a proxy of the U.S. equity markets.

S&P/TSX Index

The Canadian equivalent to the S&P 500 Index. It is also a floating market-value weighted index of the largest publicly traded companies and income trusts listed on the TSX. Unlike the S&P 500, which is balanced across all industries, the S&P/TSX Index is heavily dominated by commodity stocks, reflecting the commodities-based nature of the Canadian economy.

Target Date Funds

A type of investment fund that follows an age-based investment strategy whereby the fund changes to a more conservative asset mix as a given target date (usually retirement) nears.

TFSA

Tax-Free Savings Account—available since 2009, allows Canadians aged 18 and over to invest up to $5,000 of after-tax money. Withdrawals from a TFSA are not taxed.

Vesting

When vested, an employee has an unconditional right to a benefit (subject to locking-in restrictions). Employee contributions are always vested immediately.

Endnotes

Chapter 1

1. Ivan P. Fellegi, "On Poverty and Low Income," Statistics Canada, Ottawa, Ontario, September 1997.
2. The Organization for Economic Co-operation and Development (OECD), "Pensions at a Glance 2011: Retirement-income Systems in OECD and G20 Countries," OECD Publishing, Paris, France, March 2011.
3. Michael R. Veall, "Canadian Seniors and the Low-Income Measure," *Canadian Public Policy*, University of Toronto Press, vol. 34(s1), pages 47–58, Toronto, Ontario, November 2008.

Chapter 2

1. Statistics Canada, 2011, "Pension Plans in Canada Survey," Statistics Canada, Ottawa, Ontario, May 2012.

Chapter 3

1. Canadian Institute for Health Information (CIHI), "National Health Expenditure Trends 1975–2010," CIHI, Ottawa, Ontario, November 2010.

2. Canadian Institute for Health Information (CIHI), "National Health Expenditure Trends 1975–2010," CIHI, November 2010; and Statistics Canada, "Population by Age Group," Statistics Canada, Ottawa, Ontario, 2010.

Chapter 4

1. Alexandre Pestov, "The Elusive Canadian Housing Bubble," Schulich School of Business, Toronto, Ontario, February 2010.
2. John Krainer and Chishen Wei, "House Prices and Fundamental Value," *FRBSF Economic Letter*, Federal Reserve Bank of San Francisco, California, issue October 1, 2004.
3. Ibid.
4. For 5-year fixed rate mortgages in Canada, Bank of Canada, "Historic 5-Year Fixed Mortgage Rates."
5. Craig Wright and Robert Hogue, "Housing Trends and Affordability," RBC Economics, Royal Bank of Canada, Toronto, Ontario, March 2012.
6. Alexandre Pestov, "The Elusive Canadian Housing Bubble," Schulich School of Business, Toronto, Ontario, February 2010.
7. Number employed as a percentage of female population aged 15–64, Statistics Canada, "Labour Force Survey," Annual, Statistics Canada, Ottawa, Ontario, 2012.

Chapter 5

1. Office of the Superintendent of Financial Institutions Canada, "Canada Pension Plan Mortality Study," Actuarial Study No. 7, Ottawa, Ontario, July 2009.
2. Statistics Canada, *Spending Patterns in Canada*, Statistics Canada, catalogue 62-202-X, Ottawa, Ontario, December 2010.

Chapter 6

1. Grant Schellenberg and Yuri Ostrovsky, "General Social Survey Report," Statistics Canada, Ottawa, Ontario, 2008.
2. Statistics Canada, Winter 2011, "Perspectives on Labour and Income," Statistics Canada, Ottawa, Ontario, November 2011.

3. Julia Moulden, "Pulse No. 12—Keep on Truckin'," www.pulse.com, posted April 27, 2012.

4. TD Bank, "TD Age of Retirement Report," TD Bank Group, Toronto, Ontario, January 5, 2012.

5. BMO Retirement Institute, "Perfecting the Workplace Pension: The Quest Continues," BMO Financial Group, Toronto, Ontario, January 2012.

Chapter 7

1. TD Bank, "TD Age of Retirement Report," TD Bank Group, Toronto, Ontario, January 5, 2012.

Chapter 8

1. Statistics Canada, "Disability-free life expectancy, abridged life table, at birth and at age 65, by sex, Canada, provinces, territories, health regions and peer groups," CANSIM Table 102-0019, Statistics Canada, Toronto, Ontario.

2. Axel Borsch-Supan, "Saving and Consumption Patterns of the Elderly, The German Case," *Journal of Population Economics*, Bonn, Germany, vol. 5, no. 4, 1992.

3. Malcolm Hamilton, "The Financial Circumstances of Elderly Canadians and the Implications for the Design of Canada's Retirement Income System," *The State of Economics in Canada*, Centre for the Study of Living Studies, Ottawa, Ontario, pages 225–253, 2001.

Chapter 9

1. David A. Dodge, Alexandre Laurin, and Colin Busby, "The Piggy Bank Index: Matching Canadians' Savings Rates to Their Dreams," C.D. Howe Institute, Toronto, Ontario, March 2010.

2. Based on Statistics Canada Table 202-0703 showing average pre-tax total income divided into after-tax quintiles with figures for 2009 increased by the change in the average national wage for 2009, 2010, and 2011 to approximate 2012 quintile thresholds.

3. Department of Finance Canada, "Ensuring the Ongoing Strength of Canada's Retirement Income System," Table 1, Department of Finance, Ottawa, Ontario, 2009.

Chapter 10

1. Statistics Canada, "Household Counts by Income Quintile, Age Class, and Tenure," 2006 Census, Statistics Canada, Ottawa, Ontario.
2. Camilla Cornell, "The Real Cost of Raising Kids," *Moneysense Magazine*, Rogers Communications, Toronto, Ontario, June 2011.
3. The group whose income is higher than 60 per cent of all households with two persons or more, but lower than the top 20 per cent of such households.

Chapter 13

1. Equities, or stocks, are publicly traded securities that give you a share in a company. Shares can rise or fall in value depending on the fortunes of the company and the whims of investors. An equity fund combines investments in numerous publicly traded companies.
2. We are assuming a portfolio that is invested half in Canadian equities and half in U.S. equities (with results converted into Canadian dollars), before any fees are deducted.

Chapter 16

1. Alexandre Laurin and Finn Poschmann, "Saver's Choice: Comparing the Marginal Effective Tax Burdens on RRSPs and TFSAs," C.D. Howe Institute, Toronto, Ontario, January 27, 2010.
2. After the new rules are phased in, in 2013.

Chapter 19

1. This and the following endnotes are all from The Kaiser Family Foundation and the Health Research & Educational Trust "Employer Health Benefits Survey," Henry J. Kaiser Family Foundation, Chicago, Illinois, 2011.
2. Ibid.
3. Ibid.

Acknowledgements

The authors would like to acknowledge the invaluable contribution made by Michele Kumara in reviewing the book. Not only was Michele especially diligent in unearthing errors and inconsistencies, she also offered insightful comments that significantly improved the readability of many chapters. She dedicated many long hours to this book and made the project an enjoyable one. We also want to thank Martine Vadnais, manager of the Morneau Shepell Information Centre, who was tremendously effective in chasing down elusive data and Ling Wu-Shao who conducted research. Finally, we would like to thank the senior management of Morneau Shepell who provided both moral support as well as more tangible resources that facilitated the production of this book.

About the Authors

Fred Vettese is Chief Actuary of Morneau Shepell, a position he has held since 1991. He has written op-eds for the *National Post* and *Globe and Mail*, and is frequently quoted regarding pension matters in various media. Fred is a prolific author of pension articles for a number of magazines and journals, and has presented at various national conferences such as the Conference Board of Canada and the Canadian Institute. He is the editor and primary contributor to Morneau Shepell's newsletter, *Vision*, which gives a high level overview of major trends and issues related to retirement. Fred is a member of the C.D. Howe Institute Pension Policy Council. He graduated from the University of Toronto, became an actuary in 1980, and is a Fellow of the Canadian Institute of Actuaries (FCIA). Fred continues to provide consulting services to some of the firm's largest clients and also oversees professional standards for the firm's 150 actuaries.

Bill Morneau is Executive Chairman of Morneau Shepell. Under his leadership, the firm has become the largest Canadian human resources services firm, with over 2500 employees. Bill is Chair of the Board of Directors at St. Michael's Hospital in Toronto, and Chair of the Board of Directors at the C.D. Howe Institute. In May 2012, he was appointed by the Ontario Minister of Finance as Pension Investment Advisor, to lead in facilitating the pooling of public sector pension fund assets. Bill is also on the boards of AGF Management Ltd., the Canadian Merit Scholarship Foundation, The Learning Partnership, the London School of Economics North American Advisory Committee, the Canadian INSEAD Foundation, and Greenwood College. He is past Chair of the Board of Directors of Covenant House. In 2002, he was named as one of Canada's *Top 40 Under 40*. Bill holds a B.A. from the University of Western Ontario, an M.Sc. (Econ.) from the London School of Economics and an M.B.A. from INSEAD.

Index